COLUMBIA HEIGHTS PUBLIC LIBRARY
820 40TH AVENUE N.E.
COLUMBIA HEIGHTS, MN. 55421-2996

WITHDRAWN

MAR 2 5 2010   2010

D1116618

Your Happy Healthy Pet™

Cocker Spaniel

2nd Edition

GET MORE!
Visit www.wiley.com/
go/cockerspaniel

Liz Palika

Howell
Book House™

This book is printed on acid-free paper.

Copyright © 2009 by Wiley Publishing, Inc., Hoboken, New Jersey. All rights reserved.

Howell Book House
Published by Wiley Publishing, Inc., Hoboken, New Jersey

No part of this publication may be reproduced, stored in a retrieval system or transmitted in any form or by any means, electronic, mechanical, photocopying, recording, scanning or otherwise, except as permitted under Sections 107 or 108 of the 1976 United States Copyright Act, without either the prior written permission of the Publisher, or authorization through payment of the appropriate per-copy fee to the Copyright Clearance Center, 222 Rosewood Drive, Danvers, MA 01923, (978) 750-8400, fax (978) 646-8600, or on the web at www.copyright.com. Requests to the Publisher for permission should be addressed to the Legal Department, Wiley Publishing, Inc., 10475 Crosspoint Blvd., Indianapolis, IN 46256, (317) 572-3447, fax (317) 572-4355, or online at http://www.wiley.com/go/permissions.

Wiley, the Wiley logo, Howell Book House, the Howell Book House logo, Your Happy Healthy Pet, and related trade dress are trademarks or registered trademarks of John Wiley & Sons, Inc. and/or its affiliates in the United States and other countries, and may not be used without written permission. All other trademarks are the property of their respective owners. Wiley Publishing, Inc. is not associated with any product or vendor mentioned in this book.

The publisher and the author make no representations or warranties with respect to the accuracy or completeness of the contents of this work and specifically disclaim all warranties, including without limitation warranties of fitness for a particular purpose. No warranty may be created or extended by sales or promotional materials. The advice and strategies contained herein may not be suitable for every situation. This work is sold with the understanding that the publisher is not engaged in rendering legal, accounting, or other professional services. If professional assistance is required, the services of a competent professional person should be sought. Neither the publisher nor the author shall be liable for damages arising here from. The fact that an organization or Website is referred to in this work as a citation and/or a potential source of further information does not mean that the author or the publisher endorses the information the organization or Website may provide or recommendations it may make. Further, readers should be aware that Internet Websites listed in this work may have changed or disappeared between when this work was written and when it is read.

For general information on our other products and services or to obtain technical support please contact our Customer Care Department within the U.S. at (800) 762-2974, outside the U.S. at (317) 572-3993 or fax (317) 572-4002.

Wiley also publishes its books in a variety of electronic formats. Some content that appears in print may not be available in electronic books. For more information about Wiley products, please visit our web site at www.wiley.com.

Library of Congress Cataloging-in-Publication Data:
Palika, Liz, date.
  Cocker spaniel / Liz Palika. -- 2nd ed.
    p. cm. -- (Your happy healthy pet)
  Includes index.
  ISBN-13: 978-0-470-39060-3
  ISBN-10: 0-470-39060-3
  1. Cocker spaniels. I. Title.
  SF429.C55P346 2008
  636.752'4--dc22
                                        2008046670

Printed in the United States of America
10 9 8 7 6 5 4 3 2 1

2nd Edition

Book design by Melissa Auciello-Brogan
Cover design by Michael J. Freeland
Book production by Wiley Publishing, Inc. Composition Services

About the Author

Liz Palika has been teaching dogs and their owners in Northern San Diego County for almost twenty-five years. Her training is based on an understanding of dogs and what makes them tick. There is no funny stuff but lots of common sense.

Liz is also the author of more than fifty books; her dog training book *All Dogs Need Some Training* was listed by *Pet Life* magazine as one of the ten best dog training books available to dog owners. Liz's books have been honored with several awards from Dog Writers Association of America, Cat Writers' Association, ASPCA, Purina, and San Diego Book Writers. Liz was honored by San Diego Channel 10's Leadership Award; she was also a North County Woman of Merit. In 2005, she was awarded a Distinguished Service award from Dog Writers Association of America.

Liz is a charter member of the International Association of Canine Professionals, and is a Certified Dog Trainer (CDT) through this organization. She is also a member of the *International Association of Animal Behavior Consultants*, and an AKC CGC (Canine Good Citizen) Evaluator.

About Howell Book House

Since 1961, Howell Book House has been America's premier publisher of pet books. We're dedicated to companion animals and the people who love them, and our books reflect that commitment. Our stable of authors—training experts, veterinarians, breeders, and other authorities—is second to none. And we've won more Maxwell Awards from the Dog Writers Association of America than any other publisher.

As we head toward the half-century mark, we're more committed than ever to providing new and innovative books, along with the classics our readers have grown to love. From bringing home a new puppy to competing in advanced equestrian events, Howell has the titles that keep animal lovers coming back again and again.

Contents

Part I: The World of the Cocker Spaniel   **9**

Chapter 1: What Is a Cocker Spaniel?   **11**
What Is an American Cocker Spaniel?   11
The Cocker Spaniel's Appearance   12
Cocker Character   15

Chapter 2: Cocker Spaniels Yesterday and Today   **18**
Origins of the Breed   19
Cocker Spaniels in America   20
The Pitfalls of Popularity   23

Chapter 3: The World According to Cocker Spaniels   **24**
Are You Ready for a Dog?   24
The Pet Cocker Spaniel   26
Problems with Cocker Spaniels   31
If Cockers Could Choose Their Owners   31

Chapter 4: Choosing Your Cocker Spaniel   **32**
Breeder, Rescue, Shelter, or Free?   32
Finding the Right Cocker for You   36
Choosing Your Cocker   37
Puppy Temperament Test   40
Choosing an Adult Cocker Spaniel   41

Part II: Caring for Your Cocker Spaniel   **43**

Chapter 5: Bringing Your Cocker Spaniel Home   **44**
Puppy-Proofing Your Home and Yard   44
Puppy-Proofing Your Home   46
Basic Supplies   49
Puppy Essentials   51
When Your Dog First Comes Home   52
Pet Professionals   55

Chapter 6: Feeding Your Cocker Spaniel   **57**
Commercial Dog Foods   57
Homemade Diets   58
Feeding Your Dog   59
Reading Dog Food Labels   59

Chapter 7: Grooming Your Cocker Spaniel   **63**
Routine Care   63
Grooming Your Cocker Yourself   68
External Parasites   71
Making Your Environment Flea Free   72

Chapter 8: Keeping Your Cocker Spaniel Healthy   **75**
Health Problems Seen in Cockers   75
Know Your Dog's Normal   83
When to Call the Veterinarian   86
Internal Parasites   89
Emergency Care   92
How to Make a Canine First-Aid Kit   94
Geriatric Care   98

Part III: Enjoying Your Cocker Spaniel   **101**

Chapter 9: Training Your Cocker Spaniel   **102**
Understanding Builds the Bond   103
Practical Commands for Family Pets   109
Training for Attention   118
Teaching Cooperation   121

Chapter 10: Housetraining Your Cocker Spaniel   **122**
Your Housetraining Shopping List   122
The First Day   124
Confine Your Pup   126
Watch Your Pup   129
Accidents Happen   130
Scheduling Basics   132

**Appendix: Learning More About
Your Cocker Spaniel**   **135**
Some Good Books   135
Magazines   136
Clubs and Registries   137
On the Internet   138

Index   **141**

Shopping List

You'll need to do a bit of stocking up before you bring your new dog or puppy home. Below is a basic list of some must-have supplies. For more detailed information on the selection of each item below, consult chapter 5. For specific guidance on what grooming tools you'll need, review chapter 7.

☐ Food dish   ☐ Nail clippers

☐ Water dish   ☐ Grooming tools

☐ Dog food   ☐ Chew toys

☐ Leash   ☐ Toys

☐ Collar   ☐ ID tag

☐ Crate

There are likely to be a few other items that you're dying to pick up before bringing your dog home. Use the following blanks to note any additional items you'll be shopping for.

☐ _____

☐ _____

☐ _____

☐ _____

☐ _____

☐ _____

☐ _____

☐ _____

☐ _____

☐ _____

☐ _____

☐ _____

Pet Sitter's Guide

We can be reached at (___)_____-_____   Cellphone (___)_____-_____

We will return on _____ (date) at _____ (approximate time)

Dog's Name _____

Breed, Age, and Sex _____

Important Names and Numbers

Vet's Name _____ Phone (___)_____- _____

Address _____

Emergency Vet's Name _____ Phone (___)_____- _____

Address _____

Poison Control _____ (or call vet first)

Other individual (someone the dog knows well and will respond to) to contact in case of emergency or in case the dog is being protective and will not allow the pet sitter in. _____

Care Instructions

In the following three blanks let the sitter know what to feed, how much, and when; when the dog should go out; when to give treats; and when to exercise the dog.

Morning _____

_____

Afternoon _____

_____

Evening _____

_____

Medications needed (dosage and schedule) _____

_____

Any special medical conditions _____

_____

Grooming instructions in detail—Daily: _____

Weekly: _____

My dog's favorite playtime activities, quirks, and other tips _____

_____

Part I
The World of the Cocker Spaniel

The Cocker Spaniel

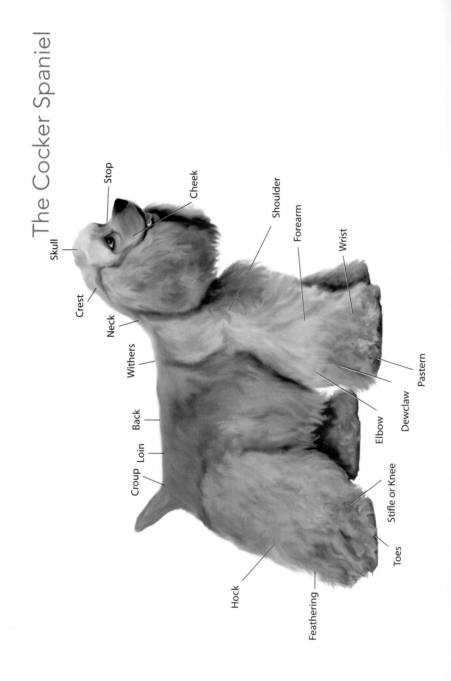

Skull
Stop
Crest
Cheek
Neck
Shoulder
Withers
Forearm
Wrist
Back
Loin
Croup
Pastern
Dewclaw
Elbow
Stifle or Knee
Toes
Hock
Feathering

Chapter 1

What Is a Cocker Spaniel?

Cocker Spaniels are perennial favorites among the dog breeds. Everyone just seems to love them. German Shepherd Dogs are recognized worldwide for their legendary working abilities, Bulldogs are instantly identified by their unique appearance, Poodles are known for their elegance, and Border Collies have exceptional intelligence. So what makes Cocker Spaniels stand out from the crowd?

Well, first of all, no one can look away from that face! With their sweet expression, large, dark eyes, and hanging ears, Cockers plant a hook in your heart right away. Then the wiggling body, wagging stub of a tail, luscious coat, and most important of all, that sparkling personality just finish you off. Once you meet a Cocker Spaniel, you become a Cocker fan.

What Is an American Cocker Spaniel?

The spaniel family of dogs is a very old one, with known records dating back as far as the fourteenth century in Europe. Many different breeds are descended from the original spaniels, including the Irish Water Spaniel, English Springer Spaniel, Welsh Springer Spaniel, Clumber Spaniel, English Toy Spaniel, Cavalier King Charles Spaniel, and English Cocker Spaniel.

The American Cocker Spaniel is now a distinctly different breed than his closest relatives, the English Springer Spaniel and the English Cocker Spaniel. This book is about the American Cocker Spaniel. The breed is also known simply as the Cocker Spaniel, and that is how he is registered with the American Kennel Club (AKC). He's also referred to as a Cocker for short.

The Cocker Spaniel's Appearance

The Cocker Spaniel is the smallest of the hunting spaniels. Although the toy spaniels (English Toy Spaniel and Cavalier King Charles Spaniel) are smaller, they are not true hunting dogs. The Cocker is also the smallest breed recognized in the AKC's Sporting Group—breeds developed to help humans hunt. Cockers stand between 13.5 and 15.5 inches tall at the withers (the top of the shoulders) and weigh between 24 and 30 pounds. Females are a bit smaller than males.

The physical description here is based on the ideal Cocker Spaniel, as set out in the breed standard (see the box on page 13). No dog meets the breed standard 100 percent. But this is the ideal that breeders strive for.

The Body

The perfect Cocker Spaniel is a small, yet sturdy and strong dog. He's a hunting dog, and should always appear ready to go for a romp in the fields. His body is slightly longer (from breastbone to the back of the hips) than he is tall (from the ground to the highest point of the shoulders).

The Cocker is a hunting spaniel and retains that heritage, as can be seen in the instinctive stance of this little puppy.

What Is a Breed Standard?

A breed standard is a detailed description of the perfect dog of that breed. Breeders use the standard as a guide in their breeding programs, and judges use it to evaluate the dogs in conformation shows. The standard is written by the national breed club, using guidelines established by the registry that recognizes the breed (such as the AKC or UKC).

Usually, the first section of the breed standard gives a brief overview of the breed's history. Then it describes the dog's general appearance and size as an adult. Next is a detailed description of the head and neck, then the back and body, and the front and rear legs. The standard then describes the ideal coat and how the dog should be presented in the show ring. It also lists all acceptable colors, patterns, and markings. Then there's a section on how the dog moves, called *gait*. Finally, there's a general description of the dog's temperament.

Each section also lists characteristics that are considered to be faults or disqualifications in the conformation ring. Superficial faults in appearance are often what distinguish a pet-quality dog from a show- or competition-quality dog. However, some faults affect the way a dog moves or his overall health. And faults in temperament are serious business.

You can read all the AKC breed standards at www.akc.org.

He has strong, straight front legs. The shoulders form an angle of about 90 degrees from the upper arm. He has moderately angled rear legs that are parallel when viewed from behind. The hips are wide and well muscled. Any dewclaws on the rear legs may be removed.

The neck is long enough to allow the dog to sniff the ground. It is muscular and clean, with little excess skin. The back is strong and slopes slightly from the shoulders to the hips. The chest is deep with plenty of room for the heart and lungs to work well when the dog is in action. The tail is docked and carried in a straight line from the back or slightly higher. It should never be straight up or tucked under.

The Head

The American Cocker Spaniel's head and face are two of the most recognizable features of the breed. The dog's expression, with large, round, dark eyes, is soft, appealing, and full of expression. The skull is rounded, the eyebrows are clearly defined, and there is a pronounced indentation between the eyes at the stop (the place where the muzzle and the skull meet).

The nose is black in black dogs, black and tans, and black and whites. In dogs of other colors, the nose may be brown, liver, or black, with darker colors preferred. The muzzle is broad and deep with square, even jaws. It should not be narrow or thin.

The head and face of the Cocker are distinctive, with the rounded skull and well-defined eyebrows.

The ears hang straight down and are well covered with hair. The ears begin on the sides of the skull no higher than the lower part of the eyes.

The Coat and Colors

The Cocker's coat is one of his crowning glories. The hair on the head is short and fine. The body has a coat of a medium length with a protective undercoat and a fine outer coat. The extra hair on the ears, chest, abdomen, and legs—called feathering—is long and luxurious. This feathering is silky flat or just slightly wavy; it should never be curly.

This breed has some very specific color varieties and patterns. Any colors or patterns other than these are not acceptable in the show ring.

- Black or black and tan: These Cockers are all black or all black with tan markings over each eye, on the sides of the muzzle, the undersides of the ears, the feet, and under the tail. A tiny bit of white is allowed on the chest or throat.
- Any solid color other than black: This color variety is abbreviated *ASCOB*. These dogs may be any solid color other than black, which includes light cream through dark red. The color must be uniform all over the dog, although the feathering may be slightly lighter. A small amount of white on the chest is allowed.

- Parti-color: Parti-color Cockers are white with patches of another color, which may include black, brown, red, cream, or roan (a mixture of colored and white hairs). The patches may also include freckles on the dog's muzzle.

Cocker Spaniels who are shown in conformation dog shows are divided into these same color varieties for the show ring. So you may see Cockers in the ring three times at the same dog show. These divisions came about based on the huge popularity of the breed at the turn of the twentieth century and the color varieties that were in demand then. In Britain in the 1800s, the red-and-white and black-and-white dogs were much more popular than solid-colored dogs, and at many dog shows only these parti-colors were exhibited. However, during the early 1900s in the United States, the black dogs were in big demand. Today, all three color varieties have their fans and all can be seen at dog shows.

His luxurious coat is one of the Cocker's most elegant features. But it does require a lot of care.

This luscious coat does require a significant amount of care. That will be discussed in chapter 7.

Gait

Gait is how a dog moves. As a well-balanced sporting dog, the Cocker possesses strength, speed, and endurance. It can be hard for a small dog to work in the field as a hunting dog, so good movement is essential. And good movement depends on correct structure.

The Cocker's muscular hips should drive him forward with power and the front legs must be able to reach easily to balance the power from the rear. In all respects, he should appear athletic and able to work in the field.

Cocker Character

Cockers have been described as merry, endearing, gentle, trusting, playful, and devoted. The Cocker Spaniel is well suited to live with people but retains a strong desire to work. Breed expert Bobbie Kolehouse says, "This is a breed developed over hundreds of years to be a gentle household companion, an intruder alarm dog, and a competent hunting partner. While many Cockers today are not used as gun dogs, those dependable traits endear them to people who love a responsive, affectionate dog." (Gun dogs were developed to help hunters find and retrieve game, often birds.)

A well-socialized Cocker Spaniel is great with kids.

They are also very responsive to their people and are an excellent barometer of the family. If the family is relaxed and happy, the Cocker will also be relaxed and happy.

However, if there is tension, anger, anxiety, or fear in the household, the dog will reflect that, too. Kolehouse says, "They are, in many ways, a measure of the emotional health of the household. Cockers are generally healthy dogs but their close connection to people makes them susceptible to chronic stress." Chronic stress can lead to behavior problems (such as barking, destructive chewing, fearful behaviors, and obsessive compulsive behaviors) as well as health issues (including self-destructive behaviors and immune system disorders).

Friends and Companions

Although bred for centuries as a hunting dog, the Cocker is also a companion dog. He is very unhappy alone and is not the dog to leave out in the backyard for hours at a time. A Cocker alone is an unhappy dog, and unhappy Cockers are likely to bark—sometimes to the point of being problem barkers and causing neighbors to complain.

An American Cocker Spaniel will enjoy a romp in the field and a chance to flush birds and chase rabbits, but at home he wants to be close to you. A Cocker is a dedicated, loyal, affection companion. He will mirror your moods—so much so that many Cocker owners find that their mood is reflected in the face of their dogs even before they recognize it themselves.

A well-socialized Cocker can be good with children. They are small enough not to be overwhelming yet sturdy enough to play with the kids. This socialization is important, though, because a Cocker who is not well-socialized can be worried, fearful, and even timid.

Trainability

Cocker Spaniels are experts at manipulating their owners. One look in those eyes and you'll understand how they do it. Training, therefore, is very important and should begin while the Cocker is a puppy. A kindergarten puppy class is a great place to begin. These classes emphasize the basic obedience commands (geared for the young puppy) and also incorporate a lot of socialization to other people and puppies.

> **TIP**
>
> **Top Dogs**
>
> In 1921, a black-and-white Cocker, Ch. Midkiff Seductive, made history by being the first Cocker Spaniel to win Best in Show at the Westminster Kennel Club Dog Show. Her owner was William T. Payne, a very famous Cocker breeder. Since then, Cockers have won at Westminster three more times. Ch. My Own Brucie won in 1940 and 1941, and Ch. Carmor's Rise and Shine won in 1954.

Housetraining the Cocker puppy requires patience. Cocker puppies are slow to develop and mature. You will need to establish a housetraining routine and schedule, and then follow it for several months. Consistency and patience are the keys here. Chapter 10 will explain more about housetraining.

When the dog and owner work together, Cockers are very trainable. However, if the Cocker is allowed to set the rules—if you fall for those expressive eyes—a Cocker Spaniel can be rude, obnoxious, and difficult to live with. A well-trained Cocker, however, is a joy.

Chapter 2

Cocker Spaniels Yesterday and Today

Spaniels have been around for a long, long time. As far back as the fourteenth century, there were dogs known as spanyells. These were hunting dogs, bred to flush game and retrieve it, and to perform a variety of other tasks for hunters. Back in that era, and for hundreds of years afterward, people hunted for sustenance, and a good versatile hunting dog (or two) could spell the difference between eating and starving. Spaniels (as we spell it today) were smaller than many other hunting dogs, and so they required less food themselves than larger hunting dogs and were easy to keep.

Spaniels were found throughout Europe in the early years, although many experts feel this family of dogs originated in Spain (from which comes the name). Before the advent of guns, in Spain the dogs worked by running back and forth (quartering) in front of their master, scenting fowl such as partridge and quail, then acted as setters, crouching to the ground to point out the birds' location. The sportsmen would send their hunting falcons up in the air, which would keep the hidden game close to the ground. Then they would go over the field with a net. If the birds tried to fly away, the hunters could shoot arrows over the dogs' heads or the falcons in the air would catch the birds.

Geoffrey Chaucer wrote about the spaniel (spelled *Spaynel*) in the late 1300s. He made it quite clear they were popular even then. William Shakespeare mentioned spaniels in many of his plays, too.

American and English Cocker Spaniels descended from the same British hunting dogs.

Origins of the Breed

The English Cocker Spaniel, the English Springer Spaniel, and those dogs that would later become the American Cocker Spaniel all share the same heritage. In fact, at one time they were all the same breed. The English Springer Spaniel Field Trial Association states that in the 1800s, "In a litter of Spaniel puppies, the smaller dogs would hunt woodcocks and were called cockers. The larger puppies in the litter were used to flush game and were therefore called springers." The cockers were said to be shorter than the springers, more compact, with a rounder head and longer ears. The most common (and popular) color was red and white, although other colors were seen. Those colors included black and white, all liver, and black and tan.

The Kennel Club was formed in Britain in 1873, and at that time efforts were made to record the histories and pedigrees of the Cockers and Springers. Although some owners and breeders had written records, the vast majority had been committed to memory. This, of course, led to mistakes, but it was a starting place for the registration of the dogs who followed.

In 1892, the Cockers and Springers were finally recognized by the Kennel Club as two different breeds. Still, many hunters continued to cross-breed the dogs for a number of years to improve their hunting abilities.

Some breed experts think the Cockers (both English and American) also have some other spaniels in their heritage, including the Cavalier King Charles Spaniel, the English Toy Spaniel, the black-and-white Dutch Spaniel, the red-and-white Italian Spaniel, and a straight-coated, web-toed, black water spaniel from France called the Pyrame.

The dog who is looked upon as the father of English Cocker Spaniels is Ch. Obo, who was whelped in 1879 in England. Obo's father was a Sussex Spaniel and his mother was a Field Spaniel (two breeds that were, in that era, closely related).

Cocker Spaniels in America

Would you believe that a spaniel arrived in New England after sailing on the Mayflower in 1620? Legends say that two dogs sailed on the Mayflower: one was a spaniel and the other was a Mastiff. Although some experts believe that spaniel was what would later be called an English Springer Spaniel, the records only call the dog a spaniel.

The first dog show in America was held in June 1874. Two black-and-tan Cocker Spaniels were shown. In those days, dogs were not registered, and individual breeders kept their own records.

Cockers became popular in North America because they were good with people and willing working dogs.

In 1878, the first Cocker Spaniel was registered with the American Kennel Club. He was a liver-and-white dog named Captain. Throughout the 1870s, all small spaniels were registered as Cockers.

The dog known today as the father of American Cocker Spaniels in America is the son of the dog considered the father of English Cocker Spaniels in Britain. Ch. Obo in Britain was bred to Ch. Chloe II, who was shipped to America when she was pregnant. She whelped a son who became Ch. Obo II. Although his conformation varied from today's dogs (he was only ten inches tall and had a very long body), he was considered an excellent dog of that era.

In the late 1800s and early 1900s, Cockers became very popular in the United States and Canada, primarily because they were very good with people, were wonderful family dogs, and yet were also willing workers in the field. They would retrieve any game they could physically carry, from doves and pigeons to geese.

The beginnings of the American Spaniel Club (the national parent club for the breed) go back to 1881, when several spaniel-owning friends formed the American Cocker Spaniel Club. It's now the oldest breed club in the United States. One of the group's first goals was to develop a breed standard.

What Is the AKC?

The American Kennel Club (AKC) is the oldest and largest pure-bred dog registry in the United States. Its main function is to record the pedigrees of dogs of the breeds it recognizes. While AKC registration papers are a guarantee that a dog is pure-bred, they are absolutely not a guarantee of the quality of the dog—as the AKC itself will tell you.

The AKC makes the rules for all the canine sporting events it sanctions and approves judges for those events. It is also involved in various public education programs and legislative efforts regarding dog ownership. The AKC has also helped establish a foundation to study canine health issues and a program to register microchip numbers for companion animal owners. The AKC has no individual members; its members are national and local breed clubs and clubs dedicated to various competitive sports.

Separating American and English Cockers

During the 1920s, some Cocker Spaniels began to change. A different physical conformation was being seen. Breed expert Lee Weston says, "The Cockers were becoming 'Americanized.'" The American dogs had a smaller muzzle, their coat was softer and silky, and they were a lighter weight. Weston says, "The differences were so striking that breeders who preferred the older type [the English type of dog] formed the English Cocker Spaniel Club in 1935." Although these enthusiasts agreed not to breed their dogs with the "Americanized" Cockers, the dogs were all shown as one breed (with the English shown as an individual variety) until 1946, when the American Kennel Club recognized the two as separate breeds.

These are English Cocker Spaniels. They're taller than American Cockers, and have longer heads and muzzles.

What's the difference? In general, American Cocker breeders today prefer a shorter-backed, smaller variety and aim for a more domed head with a shorter, plusher muzzle. The English Cocker is bigger and rangier, with a longer and narrower head, and is narrower in the chest.

Specifically, you'll see differences in the size, coat, and head between American and English Cocker Spaniels. English Cockers are a bit taller and heavier than the American breed. The American dogs tend to have a thicker, heavier coat. They also come in the popular light brown/cream color known as *buff*, a color you don't see on English Cockers.

On the head, American Cocker Spaniels have round eyes, while the English Cockers have oval eyes. The American dogs have a shorter muzzle, too. The stop, which is the spot where the muzzle meets the skull, is more abrupt on the American dogs. And the American Cockers have a rounded, almost domed head with a pronounced brow, compared to the longer and slightly flattened skull of the English Cocker.

The Proper Name

Only in the United States does the name *Cocker Spaniel* refer to the American Cocker Spaniel. In other countries, *Cocker Spaniel* or *Cocker* refers to the English Cocker Spaniel. The American type is called *American Cocker Spaniel*. A few years ago, the American Spaniel Club, which is the parent club for the Cocker Spaniel in the United States, voted on whether to change the breed name to American Cocker Spaniel. They decided not to.

The Pitfalls of Popularity

In 1936, the American Cocker Spaniel was first listed as the most popular breed registered by the American Kennel Club. The breed retained that position for the next fifty years.

The Cocker Spaniel couldn't have achieved this popularity without having many characteristics going for her. She is sturdy enough to play with the kids, yet small enough for any household. The breed's temperament is also wonderful.

However, the popularity of the breed has also been its downfall: the market has been flooded with poorly bred specimens who are timid and fearful, prone to barking, and of poor temperament. These dogs are difficult to train and handle, and more than one have bitten people. Breed

Popularity has been both kind and unkind to Cockers. They are beloved dogs, but some have also been poorly bred with more of an eye on demand than quality.

expert Lee Weston says, "As with other breeds that have attained public fame, the American Cocker Spaniel has suffered from almost devastating breeding practices by puppy mills [commercial breeders], backyard breeders, and unscrupulous dealers who saw the breed as a means of making money."

He continues, "During the past fifteen years, responsible breeders have been winning the battle to get the personality and health of the American Cocker Spaniel back to its original, loving, predictable stableness. This doesn't mean problems don't exist; they do."

You'll read more about how to find the right Cocker for you and your family in chapter 4. Just be aware that not all Cockers measure up to the ideal.

Chapter 3

The World According to Cocker Spaniels

Cocker Spaniels were originally bred as hunting dogs, and some Cockers today still do that work. However, most are primarily companion dogs. Breeder and breed expert Bonnie Kolehouse says, "This breed requires a genuine attachment to their owners. They do not like to be set aside."

Are You Ready for a Dog?

Adding a dog to your household should be a well-thought-out decision. You will be taking on the responsibility of a living, thinking, caring animal who will give you his heart. That's a big responsibility.

A dog should never be acquired on impulse. It's always best to think through what's involved in owning a dog and be honest with yourself. So let's take a look at dog ownership and see if you can do what's needed for any dog, and then we'll look specifically at Cocker Spaniels.

- Do you have time for a dog? All dogs, but especially Cockers, need your time for companionship, affection, play, and training. You cannot dash in the door, toss down some dog food, and leave again. That's not fair and the dog will react badly to it.
- Do you like to brush, comb, and groom a dog? Cockers need a great deal of coat care, and this cannot be ignored. If you don't like to do this, a Cocker may be the wrong breed for you.

Dogs are fabulous companions, but they are also a lot of work. Are you ready?

- Do you live in a place where dogs are allowed and welcome? If you rent your home, do you have permission from your landlord to have a dog? Not all neighborhoods are dog friendly, so make sure a dog will be welcome before you bring one home.
- Who, besides yourself, will be living with the dog? Is everyone in agreement to get a dog? If you want the dog but someone else in the household is afraid or doesn't like the dog, that could become very difficult.
- Is there someone in the family who could have a hard time with the dog? Is there a baby in the house, someone who is very frail, or a senior citizen with poor balance? Cockers are not large dogs but they are exuberant, especially when they're puppies.
- Do you have other pets in the household? Will your cat enjoy having a dog in the house? You may have to protect your rabbit, ferret, or gerbil from a rambunctious puppy.
- Have you lived with a dog before? Do you know what to expect? Really? Dogs can drag in dirt and leaves from outside, catch and kill a rodent, and then throw up the remains on the living room sofa.
- Do you have the money to care for a dog? Dogs need to be spayed or neutered, need vaccinations, and may hurt themselves, requiring emergency veterinary care. If you cannot do all your Cocker's grooming, you will need to pay a professional groomer every four to six weeks. Dogs need regular vet checkups, too. Plus, you will need a dog crate, leash and collar, toys, and dog food.

The Pet Cocker Spaniel

Cocker Spaniels are people dogs. Unlike other breeds, which might be happy outside sniffing out rodents or basking in the sun in the backyard, Cockers need to be inside with their people. Granted, Cockers do like to romp outside and are not averse to flushing a bird, but Cockers left outside for many hours a day will be very unhappy. This could cause barking that will annoy your neighbors or chewing that could destroy your wooden deck, the lawn furniture, or anything else in the backyard. Unhappy Cockers have also been known to be self-destructive, chewing or licking on a paw until they create a sore that will not heal.

A happy Cocker, however, is unmistakable. His smile, wiggling body, and twitching tail will tell you exactly how much he loves you.

Kids and Cocker Spaniels

Cockers can be quite patient with children, especially when they are raised with kids and are well socialized to them. Cockers are small enough not to overpower the kids and yet sturdy enough to play with them and not get hurt. However, in all fairness to the dog and for the safety of children, they should not be left alone together. Small children and puppies are not a good combination, simply because Cocker puppies are very silly and often have little self-control.

Cockers love kids and love to sleep with you. To a Cocker Spaniel, this scene is heaven.

Some people believe a puppy and a baby must grow up together for the puppy to accept the child. This is not necessarily true. Some toddlers think puppies are toys. They like to poke at the puppy's eyes or pull at his ears or maybe use the puppy to sit on. The puppy might think the toddler is something to chew. When the pup tries to defend himself by biting, he is reprimanded, although he has really only protected himself from the curious toddler.

Sleeping Habits

Cockers are usually delighted to share your bed or sleep on their own bed or crate in your bedroom. Allowing the dog to sleep in your bedroom is ideal, because then the dog gets to spend eight uninterrupted hours with you. He can hear you, smell you, and feel close to you all night. So many people have busy daytime schedules, and allowing the dog to be close at night is wonderful.

Cocker Spaniels Like Routine

If you take your Cocker for a daily morning walk, he will come to expect it and may even bring his leash to you. Your Cocker will also learn when to expect his meals, when to go to bed, and even when to expect you home from work.

Cockers are very much creatures of habit. Although this can help in some respects—housetraining is much easier on a schedule—it can have some unexpected consequences. If the schedule changes, your Cocker may be unhappy. Say, for example, you are due home from work at 5:30 but decide to stop off to visit a friend. Your Cocker will be waiting for you to come home, and when you don't show up on time he may begin to bark or he may have a housetraining accident.

Grooming Requirements

Cockers need extensive, regular grooming. That long, luscious coat needs to be combed and brushed or it will matt (tangle and form clumps). Every professional groomer can tell stories about Cockers who came in for grooming and had to be shaved down to the skin, from head to tail, because the dog was matted all over.

The long, lush coat requires daily grooming. But even Cockers who are clipped regularly need a lot of coat care.

Many pet Cockers are clipped fairly short, perhaps leaving some slight feathering (heavier hair) on the legs and belly. This coat is obviously much easier to care for than the longer coat, but it still needs to be combed.

The hair on the ears also needs to be combed or it will tangle. And often the ears need to be washed and brushed every day, because they end up in the dog's food bowl and water bowl. Grooming will be discussed in more detail in chapter 7.

Cockers Need Exercise

Cockers are not high-energy dogs but they do need moderate exercise every day. A brisk walk morning and evening is a good start, but the Cocker should also run and play. Cockers also like to retrieve, so throwing a ball is usually a favorite game. Cockers do well in many canine sports, including agility, flyball, and obviously, hunting sports.

> **Cockers Love Life**
>
> Cocker Spaniels have a definite joy about life. That merry, happy personality is a joy to behold and definitely permeates everything they do and everyone they come into contact with.

Although the Cocker has moderate exercise needs, those needs shouldn't be ignored. Exercise is necessary for maintaining good health, just as it is for keeping his human friends in their prime. In addition, Cockers are prone to obesity and exercise can help prevent that.

One way or another, your Cocker needs to be active. If you don't keep him busy, he will find ways to occupy himself.

The Dog's Senses

The dog's eyes are designed so that he can see well in relative darkness, has excellent peripheral vision, and is very good at tracking moving objects—all skills that are important to a carnivore. Dogs also have good depth perception. Those advantages come at a price, though: Dogs are nearsighted and are slow to change the focus of their vision. It's a myth that dogs are color-blind. However, while they can see some (but not all) colors, their eyes were designed to most clearly perceive subtle shades of gray—an advantage when they are hunting in low light.

Dogs have about six times fewer taste buds on their tongue than humans do. They can taste sweet, sour, bitter, and salty flavors, but with so few taste buds it's likely that their sense of taste is not very refined.

A dog's ears can swivel independently, like radar dishes, to pick up sounds and pinpoint their location. Dogs can locate a sound in $6/100$ of a second and hear sound four times farther away than we can (which is why there is no reason to yell at your dog). They can also hear sounds at far higher pitches than we can.

In their first few days of life, puppies primarily use their sense of touch to navigate their world. Whiskers on the face, above the eyes, and below the jaws are sensitive enough to detect changes in airflow. Dogs also have touch-sensitive nerve endings all over their bodies, including on their paws.

Smell may be a dog's most remarkable sense. Dogs have about 220 million scent receptors in their nose, compared to about 5 million in humans, and a large part of the canine brain is devoted to interpreting scent. Not only can dogs smell scents that are very faint, but they can also accurately distinguish between those scents. In other words, when you smell a pot of spaghetti sauce cooking, your dog probably smells tomatoes and onions and garlic and oregano and whatever else is in the pot.

The Versatile Cocker

Cockers are intelligent and are quick learners, although sometimes they can be considered a little stubborn. It can take time to undo something they have learned incorrectly. Cockers are able performers in obedience competition and love the sport of agility. Agility contests are confidence builders as well as a lot of fun.

Cockers can easily be trained for hunting and tracking. Both of these sports enable the dog and the handler to get some exercise and enjoy nature. There is nothing more rewarding than watching the Cocker use his nose. Through any of these canine sports, you will also have the opportunity to meet many wonderful people who share a common interest in your breed of choice.

Cocker Spaniels Need Socialization

Socialization is very important to this breed. Beginning early in puppyhood, Cockers should be introduced to a variety of people, and also to friendly dogs, cats, and other pets. The socialization should continue through puppyhood and on into adulthood.

Introduce your puppy as you would a stranger to a friend. Use a friendly tone of voice: "See Buddy, this is a friend," and have the person let the puppy sniff his hand. Have the friend offer the puppy a small treat. Then let the person pet the puppy while talking sweetly to him.

Look for a well-bred dog who has been properly socialized. He'll make a great pet.

Introduce other puppies and friendly adult dogs in a neutral area with both dogs on leash. Let them smell and investigate, and interrupt only if things get too rough. The puppy should be on a leash when meeting a dog-friendly cat, too, and definitely don't let the puppy chase the cat. Smaller pets (ferrets, rabbits, gerbils) should be held in your arms; let the puppy sniff them but don't let him play with or chase them.

The importance of socialization for this breed cannot be over-emphasized. A Cocker who has been isolated and not socialized will tend to be fearful, worried, timid, and may even bite out of fear.

Problems with Cocker Spaniels

Unfortunately, as with other breeds, there are some Cockers with problems. Every breed can produce a dog who may never be an enjoyable companion. Cockers who are fearful and timid are poor representatives of the breed, and may bite when they are very afraid.

Good breeders are careful to choose dogs for breeding stock who are of good temperament and personality. Unfortunately, even careful breeders can sometimes still have a problem dog. But don't take him on as a personal challenge just because you feel sorry for that dog. The risks are too great.

Although poor breeding creates some of the bad dogs we see, people can also turn a well-bred dog into a bad character. A dog who is neglected, unsocialized, teased, tormented, or treated unfairly for too long can turn into a dangerous dog.

If Cockers Could Choose Their Owners

If Cockers could choose their owners, they would probably choose someone who enjoys life as much as they do. The ability to laugh at silly things would definitely be high on the Cocker's list of owner requirements.

The owner would have to like to groom the dog and be patient while doing so. The Cocker's owner must also have creative and innovative dog training skills, as well as lots of patience. Training is important, but not all Cockers agree. The owner also has to take the time to socialize the Cocker and make sure the Cocker is well behaved in public.

Most important, the very best owner for any Cocker is one who loves their dog.

Chapter 4

Choosing Your Cocker Spaniel

There is nothing cuter than a Cocker Spaniel puppy. He is round, fuzzy, and flexible. His little tail stub is in constant motion, and his eyes are large, dark, expressive, and full of love. When you greet him, he will turn circles in delight, all the while trying to maintain eye contact. Cocker puppies are absolute joys to behold!

Cocker Spaniels can live thirteen to fifteen years. That's a long time. So when you choose a Cocker Spaniel to join your family, it's very important that you choose wisely. You want this dog to be a vital, integral part of the household. Although Cockers who have been given up by their owners can adjust to a new home, it is often very traumatic for them, because Cockers are very attached to their people.

Although most Cockers have many similar characteristics—that wonderful coat, the expressive face, and a bubbly personality—they also have individual personalities and characters. It's important that you make a well-researched choice and choose the Cocker who will best fit into your household and family.

Breeder, Rescue, Shelter, or Free?

Cockers are very popular and it's not hard to find one. I checked the classified advertisements in my local newspaper the morning I wrote this, and there were six ads for American Cocker Spaniels. I also found quite a few Cocker rescue groups on the Internet, all listing numerous dogs who need homes.

Finding the right Cocker Spaniel for you can be difficult, though. Let's take a look at some of your options.

Reputable Breeders

A breeder is someone who breeds dogs of a specific breed, in this case American Cocker Spaniels. A reputable breeder is someone who has been involved with the breed for a number of years and knows it well. They have studied the genetic and health problems in the breed and have had their dogs tested before breeding them.

They have studied the top dogs in the breed. In Cockers, hopefully, they have studied field and gun dogs as well as show dogs. Reputable breeders show their dogs, so that the judges (who are often also breeders) can independently evaluate the dogs. Some Cocker breeders also compete in other sports, including agility, obedience, and field trials, or simply go out hunting with their dogs.

Reputable breeders will also screen the people who come to buy one of their dogs. The breeder will ask potential buyers to fill out an application and may ask for personal references. The breeder will want the whole family to come for an interview, including your children. If you are not approved to buy one of their puppies, don't take it personally; the breeder

Reputable breeders give every dog they breed the best possible start in life.

is concerned about the welfare of their puppies and they know their dogs best. If they feel you are not a good match, they may be right.

When you buy a dog from a reputable breeder, you will be able to meet the mother of the litter and maybe the father, too. You will be able to ask the breeder questions, see the health tests that have been done on the sire and dam, and be able to see the entire litter as they play together. The breeder will also be available to you later, if you have any questions or problems.

Backyard Breeders

A backyard breeder is usually someone who does not have the knowledge a reputable breeder has. Many times the dog(s) being bred are simply treasured family pets and the owner breeds the dog(s) in the hopes of creating another dog just like her. Genetics doesn't work that way, though, and they end up with a litter of puppies for sale who may or may not be quality dogs.

Backyard breeders are sometimes just taking advantage of a breed's popularity in hopes of making money. Whenever a specific breed is in a popular television show or a movie, that breed's popularity usually surges. Unfortunately, many of those puppies end up in shelters, primarily because the people who bought them were expecting the dogs they saw on television or in the movies.

Puppy or adult? Both have their advantages and disadvantages.

Cocker Spaniel Rescue

When you are researching which Cocker to add to your family, keep in mind that your new dog doesn't have to be a puppy. Puppies require a great deal of time and must be housetrained (which takes a while and requires patience). Puppies also need socialization and obedience training. You might want to consider instead an older puppy, a young adult, or even a mature adult. If anyone of these sounds right to you, you may want to contact a Cocker rescue group.

Purebred rescue groups are organized by people who love their breed and are concerned about dogs who need new homes—especially those who might otherwise be killed for want of a good home. Some groups are run by breed clubs, while others are private organizations.

You will be asked to fill out an application and some groups even ask for a home visit. They want to know that your yard is fenced in, that your children will not be too rough for a Cocker, and that you and your family understand the realities of owning this breed.

Cockers in Local Shelters

A Cocker Spaniel can end up in a local shelter for many reasons. Her owner may have passed away and no one in the family wanted her. Someone may have purchased a Cocker puppy without researching the breed and, after a few months,

Cocker Spaniels end up in shelters for lots of reasons that have nothing to do with them. They can still be great pets.

realized the dog was too much for them. The dog may have escaped from the yard and was picked up as a stray and no one bailed her out. Perhaps the owner didn't realize how time-consuming the Cocker's coat care can be. There are many reasons, and many of them are not the dog's fault at all.

A Cocker in the shelter is basically an unknown. She may have been produced by a wonderful, reputable breeder or she may have come from a commercial puppy farm. Although the dog's physical appearance can give you some clues, sometimes it's really hard to tell. The dog's temperament is also an unknown, because a Cocker in a shelter is going to be very stressed and desperately unhappy; she is not going to show her real personality until she's been in a home for several months.

If you wish to save a Cocker in need, that's wonderful. Just make sure you understand the potential problems and choose the individual dog wisely. Find out as much as you can from the people who have been caring for her.

Cockers for Free

When you walk out of the grocery store and see a litter of Cocker Spaniel puppies in a cardboard box labeled, "Free to good home," think twice before taking one. Although those puppies are absolutely adorable and have eyes that melt your heart, they are probably the result of backyard breeding, maybe even an accidental breeding. The dog could be a mix; the father may even be unknown.

And although mixed-breed dogs can be great pets, you'll be disappointed if you were looking for a purebred Cocker.

The puppies (and maybe even the mother dog) may or may not have had any veterinary care, which could mean no vaccinations, no worming, and no preventive health care. The person who owned the mother dog most likely has never heard of socialization, so the puppies will not have had any planned socialization. When you get a dog from a free advertisement in the newspaper or from a box outside the store, you are getting a total unknown.

Finding the Right Cocker for You

It's not hard to find a Cocker Spaniel. It might, however, be a little more difficult to find the right dog for you. First of all, decide what the ideal Cocker would be like. Do you want to hunt with the dog? Compete in agility? Will she be a playmate for your kids or a companion for yourself? Would you like a larger dog or a slightly smaller one? Do you want an active, bubbly, extroverted Cocker, or a calmer one? Jot down some notes so you can think this through.

Then begin talking to people. Tell your family and friends what you're looking for. After all, your co-worker's neighbor may raise good Cockers and you didn't even know it. If you see a handsome, well-behaved, healthy Cocker Spaniel out on a walk, ask the owner where they got their dog.

The national and local Cocker clubs can also be a good resource, because most have a list of breeders. Do an Internet search for the American Cocker Spaniel clubs, breeders, and rescue groups in your area and contact them. You can also check the AKC web site for breeder referral contacts.

Once you have some contacts, call or e-mail the breeders and ask for an appointment to talk about their dogs. Ask the breeder a few questions: How long have you been breeding? Do you show your dogs or participate in canine sports? What health screening do you do?

You can ask the rescue group volunteer questions, too: Where do the dogs come from? How much do you know about the dogs? Are the dogs kept in a kennel or in foster homes? What kind of a behavioral evaluation is done?

The breeder or rescue volunteer will ask you questions, as well: Why do you want a Cocker? Have you owned a Cocker previously? What happened to that dog? What are your goals for this dog? What kind of training are you willing and able to do? Do you own your own home or rent? If you rent, do you have your landlord's permission to get a dog? Will the dog live in the house or outside? Are

Start your temperament test by looking at the whole litter and how the pups interact.

you able to do the grooming Cockers require? The answers to these and other questions will determine whether the breeder or rescue group will let you have one of their dogs.

Choosing Your Cocker

Service dog trainers have developed puppy tests that help them evaluate puppies' responses to specific stimuli. This helps them choose puppies for certain kinds of service dog work. The service dog trainers are then able to train only those dogs who have the temperament, character, and personality traits that are best suited for the specific work. This enables them to focus their efforts on dogs who are best able to complete the training program.

Puppy tests can help you, too, because you can use them to choose the best dog for you, your family, and your goals. The tests are best done when the puppy is 6 to 7 weeks old. Many breeders do puppy tests, and if your dog's breeder does, ask if you can watch. If the breeder normally doesn't test the puppies, ask if you can do it. They may be interested enough in the results to say yes.

To get started, list all the puppies on a sheet of paper. If several look alike, put different colored ribbons or different collars on them.

Look at the Whole Litter

Without getting involved (no petting right now), just watch the entire litter. By 6 weeks of age, the puppies will be playing with one another, bouncing around, tripping over each other and their own clumsy paws. Make some notes about their behavior.

The boldest puppy, who is often also the biggest, is usually the first to do anything. She is the first to the food, the first to check out a new toy, and the first to investigate anything new. This is a good field or gun dog puppy or perhaps an agility competition puppy. She would not be a good choice for someone who lives alone and works long hours, nor would she be a good dog for someone who is uncomfortable in a leadership role with their dog.

The fearful puppy will sit in a corner by herself, just watching what her brothers and sisters are doing. Her tail will be tight to her hindquarters and she may duck her head. Unfortunately, fearful, neurotic Cockers are not unknown. Although some fearful puppies can come out of their shell with a calm, caring, knowledgeable owner, these dogs usually retain some of their fear all their lives. These dogs are not good for noisy, active households or for first-time dog owners. Even with a knowledgeable owner, these dogs can often be a problem.

Most puppies fall somewhere between these two extremes. In one situation, the puppy may be bold and outgoing, and in another, she may fall back to

In the end, you must listen to your heart as well as your head in choosing the right dog for you.

watch. While you're watching, look to see who is the crybaby, who is the troublemaker, and who always gets the toy. Jot down notes.

Now it's time for the test. You'll find it in the box on page 40.

Looking at the Results

There are no right or wrong answers. This is only a guide to help you choose the right puppy for you. Puppies can change as they grow up.

The puppy who scored mostly A's is a middle of the pack dog in terms of dominance. This is not the most dominant puppy nor the most submissive. If she also scored an A in the ball test, this puppy will suit most families with children or active couples. She should accept training well, and although she may have some challenges during adolescence, she should grow up to be a nice dog.

The puppy who scored mostly A's and B's will be a little more dominant, a little more pushy. If she scored a B or a D on the ball test, you may find training to be somewhat of a challenge.

The puppy who scored mostly B's is a more dominant puppy. She could be a great field or gun dog or an agility or performance sports dog with the right owner. She needs an owner who has a more forceful personality; she is not the right dog for a passive person. She will need structured training from puppyhood on into adulthood.

The puppy who scored mostly C's will need special handling because this puppy is very worried about life. If pushed too far, she could bite out of fear. She needs a calm environment and a calm, confident owner.

The puppy who scored C's and D's may have trouble bonding with people. However, if she finds the right owner, she will bond and will be very devoted. This puppy needs calm, careful, patient training.

The puppy who scored mostly D's doesn't think she needs people. She is very self-confident and will need to spend a lot of time with her owner so she can develop a relationship. If she spends too much time alone, she may not bond with a person at all.

Now What?

After looking at the puppies, testing them all, figuring out the results, and perhaps narrowing the litter down to two or three puppies, what's next? Although these tests can help narrow your choices, you still need to listen to your heart. Which face really appeals to you? Which puppy climbed into your lap and refused to get down? Use the test results to help you, and then use your heart to choose that one puppy who will be best suited for you and your family.

Puppy Temperament Test

Have your paper at hand and make notes as you go along, or better yet, have someone else make notes for you. Test each puppy individually. Don't look at your notes until you're done.

Walk away. Place the puppy on the ground at your feet. Stand up and walk away. Does the puppy:

a. Follow you.
b. Put herself underfoot, climbing on your feet.
c. Do a belly crawl to follow you.
d. Ignore you and go the other direction.

Call the puppy. Move away from the puppy, then bend over and call her, spreading your hands and arms wide to encourage her. Does the puppy:

a. Come to you, tail wagging.
b. Chase you so fast that you don't have a chance to call her.
c. Come slowly or crawl on her belly to you.
d. Ignore you.

Gentle restraint. Pick up the puppy and gently roll her over so she's on her back in your arms. Place a hand on her chest to gently restrain her for thirty seconds—no longer. Does she:

a. Struggle for a few seconds, then relax.
b. Struggle for the entire thirty seconds.
c. Cry, tuck her tail up, and perhaps urinate.
d. Struggle for fifteen seconds, stop, then look at you or look away.

Lifting. When the puppy is on the ground, place both hands under her ribcage and lift her paws off the ground for thirty seconds. Does the puppy:

a. Quietly accept it with just a little wiggling.
b. Struggle for at least fifteen seconds.
c. Accept it with a tucked tail.
d. Struggle for more than fifteen seconds.

Toss a ball. With the puppy close to you, show her a ball and then toss it just a few feet away. Does the puppy:

a. Dash after it, pick it up, and bring it back to you.
b. Bring it back but doesn't want to give it back to you.
c. Go after it but does not pick it up, or gets distracted.
d. Pick it up but walk away.

Choosing an Adult Cocker Spaniel

Unfortunately, puppy tests do not work on adult dogs. Adult dogs come with a history, they have learned to interact with people, and they know that people may expect certain things. In a stressful situation such as a shelter or a foster home, the dog may react in a way she normally would not.

First of all, find out as much as you can about the dog you're looking at. Ask the shelter or rescue volunteer why she was given up. Because of privacy laws they might not be able to give you any personal details, but they should be able to tell you whether she was a stray or was given up by her owner. She may have been brought in because her owner passed away and no one in the family wanted her.

Ask how she gets along with other dogs, how she relates to cats, and if she chases birds and squirrels. Does she like children? Is she housetrained? Does she bark? Have they seen any other potential problems? Has she had any obedience training at all?

Then ask if you can spend some time with her. Take her for a walk. Sit on the grass and let her get to know you. If you've brought your family with you to meet her, make sure the kids are calm and quiet so they don't scare her. Be aware, too, that this dog may be grieving. Cockers are very attached to their people and, when removed from their previous home and family, they will grieve.

An adult dog can make a great pet. What you see is what you get, so spend some time getting to know the dog.

You might even be able to take her home for a weekend so you can see her in your home environment. Just realize that she will be stressed. If you adopt her, you won't see her true personality for several weeks.

Part II

Caring for Your Cocker Spaniel

Chapter 5

Bringing Your Cocker Spaniel Home

Adding a new puppy to the family is very exciting. This new dog will be your companion and best friend for the next thirteen to fifteen years. Unfortunately, this can also be a difficult time. Puppies can create havoc and your normal routine will be disrupted. You can make some preparations ahead of time that will make this transition easier. These arrangements will also help ensure your new puppy's safety as he joins your family.

Puppy-Proofing Your Home and Yard

Puppies will get into everything. After all, they have no idea that many of the things in our homes and yards can be dangerous. Getting into the cleaning stuff under the kitchen sink can be deadly, and chewing on electrical cords could cause the puppy to be shocked and could even burn down your house!

Puppies also have no concept that there's a difference between that leather rawhide you give them to chew and your new leather shoes. Kate Abbott, a trainer for Kindred Spirits Dog Training in Vista, California, says, "Preventing problems from happening is a much more effective training technique than allowing the dog to get into trouble and then trying to fix the behavior later. By puppy-proofing your house and yard and putting away everything you don't want the puppy to get in to, you can prevent him from getting into trouble."

Abbott adds, "Keep in mind, bad behaviors can be self-rewarding. As far as the puppy is concerned, it's fun to get into the trash can because there may be good stuff in there. And if a bad behavior is self-rewarding, the puppy will continue to do it and it will quickly turn into a bad habit."

Home Safety

The box on page 46 will go into detail about what to look for when you're making your home safe for your new dog. Just keep in mind that your new Cocker has no idea what is expensive and what is dangerous and what has sentimental value to you. A puppy especially explores the world with his nose and mouth. So when something smells good—like your leather shoes or the trash in the kitchen—he's going to want to check it out.

That sense of smell also comes into play when an item smells like you. As the puppy bonds with you, he's going to associate your smell—your personal odor—with security, safety, food, and play. So any item that smells like you, including the TV remote, your cell phone, your purse or wallet, your dirty underwear and socks, and your shoes, will attract the puppy. That's why so many remotes and cell phones get chewed up by puppies. Get into the habit of picking things up and putting them away.

Puppies will chew up whatever they can get their teeth on. Pick up and put away the things you don't want your new dog to chew.

Puppy-Proofing Your Home

You can prevent much of the destruction puppies can cause and keep your new dog safe by looking at your home and yard from a dog's point of view. Get down on all fours and look around. Do you see loose electrical wires, cords dangling from the blinds, or chewy shoes on the floor? Your pup will see them too!

In the kitchen:
- Put all knives and other utensils away in drawers.
- Get a trash can with a tight-fitting lid.
- Put all household cleaners in cupboards that close securely; consider using childproof latches on the cabinet doors.

In the bathroom:
- Keep all household cleaners, medicines, vitamins, shampoos, bath products, perfumes, makeup, nail polish remover, and other personal products in cupboards that close securely; consider using childproof latches on the cabinet doors.
- Get a trash can with a tight-fitting lid.
- Don't use toilet bowl cleaners that release chemicals into the bowl every time you flush.
- Keep the toilet bowl lid down.
- Throw away potpourri and any solid air fresheners.

In the bedroom:
- Securely put away all potentially dangerous items, including medicines and medicine containers, vitamins and supplements, perfumes, and makeup.
- Put all your jewelry, barrettes, and hairpins in secure boxes.
- Pick up all socks, shoes, and other chewables.

In the rest of the house:
- Tape up or cover electrical cords; consider childproof covers for unused outlets.
- Knot or tie up any dangling cords from curtains, blinds, and the telephone.

- Securely put away all potentially dangerous items, including medicines and medicine containers, vitamins and supplements, cigarettes, cigars, pipes and pipe tobacco, pens, pencils, felt-tip markers, craft and sewing supplies, and laundry products.
- Put all houseplants out of reach.
- Move breakable items off low tables and shelves.
- Pick up all chewable items, including television and electronics remote controls, cell phones, shoes, socks, slippers and sandals, food, dishes, cups and utensils, toys, books and magazines, and anything else that can be chewed on.

In the garage:
- Store all gardening supplies and pool chemicals out of reach of the dog.
- Store all antifreeze, oil, and other car fluids securely, and clean up any spills by hosing them down for at least ten minutes.
- Put all dangerous substances on high shelves or in cupboards that close securely; consider using childproof latches on the cabinet doors.
- Pick up and put away all tools.
- Sweep the floor for nails and other small, sharp items.

In the yard:
- Put the gardening tools away after each use.
- Make sure the kids put away their toys when they're finished playing.
- Keep the pool covered or otherwise restrict your pup's access to it when you're not there to supervise.
- Secure the cords on backyard lights and other appliances.
- Inspect your fence thoroughly. If there are any gaps or holes in the fence, fix them.
- Make sure you have no toxic plants in the garden.

Make Your Yard Safe

Cocker Spaniels are companion dogs and prefer to spend all of their time with you. However, Cockers are still field dogs and also enjoy a romp outside. They will watch the birds and try to chase them, hunt for squirrels, and may even chase butterflies. It's also important that your Cocker spend some time away from you once in a while, even when you're at home, so that he doesn't panic when he is left alone. Cockers can develop separation anxiety and this behavior can be very difficult to treat and change. So if your home situation allows it, let him go outside without you every day for forty-five minutes or an hour.

A secure fence is very important. Although Cockers are not usually efficient climbers and rarely go over a five- or six-foot-high fence, they will dig under a fence if they can. Therefore, the fence should go all the way to the ground (or even underground) and there should be no gaps between the fence and the ground. If there are gaps, fasten some wire fencing (hardware cloth is fine) to the fence and then fill the gap with the fencing. Or bend it when it reaches the ground so it extends into your yard. Use tent pegs or anchors to hold this fencing to the ground.

A solid fence that the dog cannot see through is best. Cockers can be barkers, and if the dog can see through the fence, he's going to be more apt to bark as people and other dogs walk by. Unfortunately, this can lead to problem barking.

Don't forget to make your yard safe and secure for your dog.

A solid fence can also prevent people—especially children—from putting their fingers through the fence. Cockers are cute and everyone likes to pet them. But a dog behind the fence might feel like he needs to protect his yard and fingers poked through the fence could get nipped.

If your fence is not secure or if you would like to protect some parts of your yard, you can build a dog run. A dog run should be large enough to provide your dog with space to move around and room to relieve himself away from his favorite place to bask in the sun. Since Cockers can be diggers, the floor of the run should be concrete or should have wire fencing under the dirt or sand substrate.

Your dog should always have some shade and shelter from the weather, no matter whether he's in the entire yard or in a dog run. This can be a shade awning, a large tree, or even access to the garage. Very few Cockers will use a dog house, so this will be wasted.

He should also have a source of fresh, clean water. A five-gallon galvanized tub works well because it's large enough that the water can stay cool and heavy enough that the dog cannot tip it over.

Do you have a pool? Make sure the dog is either in a run, safely away from the pool, or the pool is securely fenced. You may want to talk to a local dog trainer about how to teach your Cocker to get out of the pool if he jumps in or falls in accidentally. But you still need to keep the pool well secured, fenced off and/or covered when you're not around to supervise.

Before you bring your new dog home, walk around your yard trying to look at it from either a puppy's viewpoint or, if you're bringing home an adult dog, that dog's viewpoint. Is the fence secure? Are there any gaps under the fence that could become escape holes? Are there any plants in the backyard that you want to protect from a puppy's antics? Are the kids' toys put away? Is there anything out in the yard the dog can hurt himself on (pool supplies, gardening equipment, poisonous plants, or toxic substances)? Preventing problems is better for you, your dog, and of course, your budget.

Basic Supplies

The box on page 51 outlines most of the basics you will need for your dog, although the breeder or rescue group may also supply you with a shopping list. I will discuss dog foods in detail in chapter 6, but for now, just plan on having a supply on hand of the food the dog has been eating. If you decide to change foods, you'll want to do that very gradually so your new dog doesn't end up with a tummyache. I'll also talk about grooming in more detail in chapter 7, so right now, just pick up some basic tools. You can always get special grooming tools later.

Chew toys are high on the list of items every dog needs.

Identification

You will want to put some identification on your new dog right away. Get a tag and just make sure your phone numbers (home and cell) are on the dog's tag. You don't even need to know the dog's name yet; you can get one with his name later. Put the tag on a buckle collar (nylon or leather) that will be on him all the time. If you're bringing home a puppy, you'll have to replace that collar a couple of times as he grows.

Put an identification tag on your new dog right away.

Your New Cocker's Name

If you are bringing home a new puppy, you will be able to name him. Some people already have a name in mind, while others like to get to know the dog first. Many owners like to match the dog's personality or another characteristic with his name.

Puppy Essentials

You'll need to go shopping *before* you bring your puppy home. There are many, many adorable and tempting items at pet supply stores, but these are the basics.

- **Food and water dishes.** Look for bowls that are wide and low or weighted in the bottom so they will be harder to tip over. Stainless steel bowls are a good choice because they are easy to clean (plastic never gets completely clean) and almost impossible to break. Avoid bowls that place the food and water side by side in one unit—it's too easy for your dog to get his water dirty that way.
- **Leash.** A six-foot leather leash will be easy on your hands and very strong.
- **Collar.** Start with a nylon buckle collar. For a perfect fit, you should be able to insert two fingers between the collar and your pup's neck. Your dog will need larger collars as he grows up.
- **Crate.** Choose a sturdy crate that is easy to clean and large enough for your puppy to stand up, turn around, and lie down in. You will need either a large crate that can be sectioned off while your puppy is small or you'll need to get a couple different crates as he grows up.
- **Nail cutters.** Get a good, sharp pair that are the appropriate size for the nails you will be cutting. Your dog's breeder or veterinarian can give you some guidance here.
- **Grooming tools.** Different kinds of dogs need different kinds of grooming tools. See chapter 7 for advice on what to buy.
- **Chew toys.** Dogs *must* chew, especially puppies. Make sure you get things that won't break or crumble off in little bits, which the dog can choke on. Very hard rubber bones are a good choice. Dogs love rawhide bones, too, but pieces of the rawhide can get caught in your dog's throat, so they should only be allowed when you are there to supervise. Chew toys must be large enough that the dog cannot inadvertently swallow them.
- **Toys.** Watch for sharp edges and unsafe items such as plastic eyes that can be swallowed. Many toys come with squeakers, which dogs can also tear out and swallow. The toys, including balls, should be large enough so the dog cannot choke on them. All dogs will eventually destroy their toys; as each toy is torn apart, replace it with a new one.

Choose your dog's name wisely, though. If you give him a name that is based on a current celebrity, will you still like that name in ten or thirteen years? The same goes with a silly puppy name. If you call the dog Baby or Puppers, will that still be suitable when the dog is grown up?

Also, choose one that you won't be embarrassed to call out in public!

When Your Dog First Comes Home

You're going to be excited when you first bring home your new Cocker, and chances are, you're going to want to share that excitement. Restrain yourself right now for your new dog's sake. Although Cockers are very social dogs, they do get upset at changes. In addition, they bond strongly with their people and your new dog may be grieving for his previous owner or his breeder and litter-mates. Your new best friend needs time to get to know you and bond with you before he meets other people.

It's important for your dog to meet all kinds of people, but take it slow the first week. Keep him home and give him time to get to know your family.

Bonding is the process of developing a relationship. When he is bonded with you, he will care about you and will want to be with you. When you are bonded with him, you will do anything to keep him safe. This bonding takes a little time, so be selfish and keep him at home with you and your family for a week or so.

Later it will be important for him to meet your neighbors, friends, and extended family so he can become socialized to other people. Just keep the get-togethers brief and control the meetings. Don't let people get rough with the puppy, even in play, and let just one or two people meet him at a time. Never let a group of people gang up on him; even the most social Cocker could be frightened by that.

Crate Training

Adding a Cocker Spaniel puppy or dog to your household can be a wonderful experience, but it can sour quickly if the dog is ruining your carpets and chewing up your shoes. There is a training tool on the Puppy Essentials list that can help—a crate. Two types of crates are commonly used. The first is a heavy plastic molded carrier, much like those the airlines require. The second is made of heavy metal wire bars. The choice of which to use is strictly a personal preference, but whichever you choose should be large enough for an adult dog to stand up, turn around, and lie down.

A crate enables you to use the dog's natural denning instinct, the instinct that causes dogs to curl up behind the chair or under a table when they nap. Puppies also have a natural instinct not to relieve themselves in the place where they sleep.

At first, supervise your dog and limit the amount of space he has in the house. He is learning every moment, so make sure he doesn't learn bad habits.

A crate helps housetrain a puppy by using that instinct.

Introduce the crate to your puppy by opening the door and tossing a treat or toy inside. Allow the puppy to come and go as he pleases and to investigate the crate. When he is going in and out after a few treats, give him a treat and close the door. Leave the door closed for a few minutes and then let the puppy out—if, and only if, he is being quiet. If the puppy is throwing a temper tantrum, don't let him out. If you do, you will have taught your puppy that a temper tantrum works to get him what he wants.

Put the puppy in his crate when you are home and can't supervise him or when you are busy, such as eating a meal. Put the puppy in the crate when he is overstimulated—time-outs are good for puppies, too. And of course, put the puppy in his crate for the night.

Never leave the puppy in the crate longer than four hours, except at night when the crate is next to your bed. It takes a while for the puppy to develop good bowel and bladder control, and you need to be able to let the puppy out when it's time to eliminate. Crate training will be discussed in more detail in chapter 9.

Supervise Your Dog

As I've mentioned previously, many of the commonly seen problems with dogs can be avoided through simple prevention. Supervising the dog is one means of prevention. Your Cocker can't chew up your sofa if you supervise him while he's in the house with you and you put him in his crate or outside in his pen when you can't watch him. By supervising the dog, you can teach him what is allowed and what is not.

Using the sofa as an example, if your Cocker puppy decides to take a nibble out of the sofa cushion and you are paying attention, you can tell the puppy, "Aack! No!" as he grabs the cushion. Then you follow through by handing your puppy one of his chew toys: "Here, chew this instead."

The same can occur with food. As I said in previous chapters, Cockers love food and even when they're well fed they will try to steal any food they can find. By practicing prevention—putting away food, keeping things picked up, and putting the cat's food out of the dog's reach—you can stop bad behavior before it happens. You can also prevent potential problems, such as gastrointestinal upset from eating too many of the wrong things.

Time with Your Dog

As I have mentioned several times, Cockers are very people-oriented and must spend time with their owners. Your dog should be inside with you when you are home and next to your bed (in his crate) at night, except for his trips outside to

Set aside time to spend with your dog. He just wants to be with you.

relieve himself. In addition, you will need to make time to play with your dog, train him, and make sure he gets enough exercise.

With a little thought, it's amazing how creative people can be with their schedules. To spend time with your dog in the morning, getting up thirty minutes earlier will give you time for a fifteen- to twenty-minute walk before taking your shower. If you work close to home, your lunch hour might be just enough time to get home and eat your lunch as you throw the Frisbee for your dog. In the evening, take the children with you as you walk the dog. You can find out what's going on with the kids as you exercise and train your dog.

Pet Professionals

Enlisting the help of some experienced pet professionals can help you keep your dog healthy, well behaved, and well cared for throughout his lifetime.

Veterinarian

The veterinarian to whom you choose to give your business will become your partner in your dog's continued good health. Like a family physician, the veterinarian will get to know your dog, keep records on his weight and physical condition, and help you get your dog through any health challenges.

When choosing a vet, call and make an appointment to go in without your dog. Expect to pay for this office call, since you are taking up the vet's time. Then ask some questions. The first one should be, "Do you like Cockers?" If your vet has had some bad experiences with the breed, they may prefer not to work with them. You don't want someone taking care of your dog who dislikes the breed or who is afraid of them.

Choose a veterinarian for your dog before you bring him home.

If the veterinarian likes the breed, ask about their veterinary experience, office practices, and policies. What problems do they normally see with the breed and how do they handle those issues? How do they handle emergencies or after-hours problems?

When you have had a thorough discussion with the vet and it seems the two of you will be able to work together, make another appointment for your dog. You want to make sure your new dog is healthy and get him started on vaccinations and other health-care needs.

Trainer

Just as with the veterinarian, find a trainer who likes Cockers. Ask about their experience with the breed, what problems they have seen, and how they handle them. If you see a well-behaved, nicely trained Cocker when you are out for a walk, ask where the owner took their dog for training.

Every trainer has their own training technique, so watch one of this trainer's classes or training sessions without your dog. Make sure you will be happy with their training style and technique before you sign up for classes.

Groomer

If you don't feel comfortable giving your Cocker Spaniel regular haircuts—and most Cocker owners don't have those skills—you will want to find a professional groomer. You can find a groomer by asking around. If you have friends or neighbors with Cockers, ask where they take their dog for grooming and whether they are satisfied with the results. Do their dogs like going into the groomer's facility or are they hesitant? You can also ask for referrals from your veterinarian or from a local dog trainer.

When choosing a professional groomer, check out how well they get along with Cockers. Some ill-tempered dogs don't appreciate having mats combed out; consequently, some groomers prefer not to bother with the breed. A groomer may not like Cockers, and if the dog senses the animosity, the problem will be compounded. So choose a groomer who likes the breed and works with quite a few of them.

Most groomers recommend that Cockers come in for an appointment every four weeks. If you keep up with your dog's coat in between appointments, then visit the groomer once a month, you will keep your dog looking healthy, clean, and well cared for.

Chapter 6

Feeding Your Cocker Spaniel

Make sure you ask your dog's breeder or the rescue volunteer what food your new Cocker Spaniel has been eating. Even if you prefer a different food, feed your dog the food she is used to for the first few weeks after she comes home. Then, when she's beginning to adjust to the changes in her life, you can slowly begin changing her food.

Cockers can be sensitive to changes around them, including changes in foods. So if you decide to change your dog's food, do so very slowly. Add one-third new food to two-thirds old food for the first week, then half new and half old the second week, and two-thirds new and one-third old on the third week. By the end of a month, your Cocker should be eating her new food with no gastrointestinal upsets. If at any time your Cocker has soft stools, make the change even more slowly.

Commercial Dog Foods

Dog food sales in the United States are a huge business with tremendous competition among manufacturers. Dog owners should understand that as a big business, these companies' goals include making a profit. Although advertising may show a dog and owner in a warm and fuzzy, heart-tugging moment, the nutrition your dog might get from the food being advertised has nothing to do with that heart-tugging moment. It's all about getting you to buy the food.

Dog owners must be wise consumers, and we cannot let the pet food recall of 2007 fade from memory. Read the dog food labels, check out the manufacturers'

When choosing a commercial dog food, read the label carefully and choose a complete and balanced diet made with plenty of meat.

web sites, check the recall lists, and talk to dog food experts, including your veterinarian if they have a background in nutrition.

A good-quality food is necessary for your Cocker's health. Dog foods vary in quality, from the very good to the terrible. To make sure you are using a high-quality food, read the labels on the packages (see the box on page 59). Make sure the food offers the levels of protein, carbohydrates, and fats recommended earlier in this chapter.

Read the list of ingredients, too. If one of the first ingredients listed is by-products, be wary of the food. By-products are the parts of slaughtered animals that are not muscle meat and usually include lungs, spleen, kidneys, brain, liver, blood, bone, fatty tissue, stomach, and intestines. Dog food manufacturers can meet protein requirements by including by-products, but they are inferior forms of protein that do not metabolize as completely in the dog's body.

Cockers do well on a dog food that uses a muscle meat as the first ingredient. Muscle meats are listed on the label simply as beef, chicken, fish, and so on.

Homemade Diets

Dog owners who feed homemade diets usually do so because they are concerned about the quality of commercially available foods. Some owners do not want their dogs eating the additives or preservatives that are in many commercial dog foods. Others cook their dog's food so they can control exactly what their dogs eat. Many, many people began making homemade diets for their dogs during and after the pet food recalls of 2007.

There are many resources now available to dog owners who wish to feed a homemade diet. Just make sure the diet is complete and contains all the nutrients your dog needs. Keep a line of communication open with your veterinarian so they can monitor your dog's continued good health.

Reading Dog Food Labels

Dog food labels are not always easy to read, but if you know what to look for they can tell you a lot about what your dog is eating.

- The label should have a statement saying the dog food meets or exceeds the American Association of Feed Control Officials (AAFCO) nutritional guidelines. If the dog food doesn't meet AAFCO guidelines, it can't be considered complete and balanced, and can cause nutritional deficiencies.
- The guaranteed analysis lists the minimum percentages of crude protein and crude fat and the maximum percentages of crude fiber and water. AAFCO requires a minimum of 18 percent crude protein for adult dogs and 22 percent crude protein for puppies on a dry matter basis (that means with the water removed; canned foods will have less protein because they have more water). Dog food must also have a minimum of 5 percent crude fat for adults and 8 percent crude fat for puppies.
- The ingredients list the most common item in the food first, and so on until you get to the least common item, which is listed last.
- Look for a dog food that lists an animal protein source first, such as chicken or poultry meal, beef or beef byproducts, and that has other protein sources listed among the top five ingredients. That's because a food that lists chicken, wheat, wheat gluten, corn, and wheat fiber as the first five ingredients has more chicken than wheat, but may not have more chicken than all the grain products put together.
- Other ingredients may include a carbohydrate source, fat, vitamins and minerals, preservatives, fiber, and sometimes other additives purported to be healthy.
- Some brands may add artificial colors, sugar, and fillers—all of which should be avoided.

Feeding Your Dog

Some dog owners like to fill a bowl of dog food and leave it out all day, letting the dog munch at will. Although it may be convenient, it is not a good idea, for several reasons. First of all, outdoors the bowl of food may attract birds, squirrels, and ants. Indoors, the food may attract ants, flies, and cockroaches. In addition, the food could become rancid.

When you are housetraining your puppy, free feeding makes it difficult to set up a routine. Your puppy will need to relieve herself after eating, and if she munches all day long, you won't be able to tell when she should go outside.

> **TIP**
>
> Don't forget to wash your dog's bowl after each meal. The leftover food particles and her saliva can cause bacteria buildup in the bowl. Although she may not get sick right away, if the bacteria continue to build, she will. The water bowl should be cleaned regularly, too.

Last, but certainly not least, psychologically your dog needs to know that you are the giver of the food. How better for her to learn it than when you hand her a bowl several times a day? If the food is always available, you are not the one giving it. It's always just there—at least as far as your dog is concerned.

When you put the food bowl down for regular meals, your dog knows that you are the one who feeds her.

How Much?

Each Cocker Spaniel needs a different amount of food. When puppies are growing quickly, they will need more food. When your Cocker is all grown up, if she continues eating that same amount of food, she will get fat. The dog's individual body metabolism, activity rate, and lifestyle all affect her nutritional needs.

Most dog food manufacturers print a chart on the bag showing how much to feed your dog. It's important to remember that these are *suggested* guidelines. If your puppy or dog is soft, round, and fat, cut back on the food. If your dog is thin and always hungry, give her more food. A healthy, well-nourished dog will have bright eyes, an alert expression, a shiny coat, supple skin, and energy to work and play.

Pet Food vs. People Food

Many of the foods we eat are excellent sources of nutrients—after all, we do just fine on them. But dogs, like us, need the right combination of meat and other ingredients for a complete and balanced diet, and a bowl of meat doesn't provide that. In the wild, dogs eat the fur, skin, bones, and guts of their prey, and even the contents of the stomach.

This doesn't mean your dog can't eat what you eat. A little meat, dairy, bread, some fruits, or vegetables as a treat are great. Just remember, we're talking about the same food you eat, not the gristly, greasy leftovers you would normally toss in the trash. Stay away from sugar, too, and remember that chocolate and alcohol are toxic to dogs.

If you want to share your food with your dog, be sure the total amount you give her each day doesn't make up more than 15 percent of her diet, and that the rest of what you feed her is a top-quality complete and balanced dog food. (More people food could upset the balance of nutrients in the commercial food.)

Can your dog eat an entirely homemade diet? Certainly, if you are willing to work at it. Any homemade diet will have to be carefully balanced, with all the right nutrients in just the right amounts. It requires a lot of research to make a proper homemade diet, but it can be done. It's best to work with a veterinary nutritionist.

Mealtimes

Most experts recommend that puppies eat two to three times a day. Most adult dogs do very well with two meals, ten or twelve hours apart, so feed your dog after you eat breakfast and then again after you have dinner.

While you are eating, don't feed your Cocker from the table or toss her scraps. This will teach her to beg from anyone at the table—a very bad habit. Don't toss her leftovers as you are cooking, either. That can lead to begging and even stealing in the kitchen. Cockers are bright enough to figure out how to open cupboard doors and are bold enough to raid the kitchen trash can.

A fat dog is not healthy. Feed your dog nutritious snacks in moderate amounts and keep her active and in good weight.

Treats

An occasional dog biscuit or some training treats will not spoil your Cocker's appetite, but don't get in the habit of offering treats just for the pleasure of it. Many dogs are overweight and obesity is a leading killer of dogs. Unfortunately, with their ever-present appetite and their love of comfort, Cockers do tend to gain weight easily.

When you offer treats, offer either treats made specifically for dogs or something that is nutritious and low in calories, like a carrot. Don't offer candy, cookies, leftover tacos, or anything like that. Your Cocker doesn't need sugar, chocolate is deadly for dogs, and spicy foods can cause diarrhea and an upset stomach. Play it safe and give your Cocker good-quality, nutritious snacks very sparingly.

If you are using treats to train your dog, use good ones—nutritious treats—and cut back on all other treats. Training treats can be pieces of cooked meats such as chicken or beef. Just dice up the pieces very small. Cheese is also a great training treat. Cut it into tiny pieces, put it in a sandwich bag, and toss it in the freezer. Bring out a few frozen pieces for each training session. (Cheese is easy to handle when frozen, and your dog won't mind.)

Chapter 7

Grooming Your Cocker Spaniel

T he Cocker Spaniel is an appealing and beautiful dog, and regular grooming will help keep him looking his best. In addition, regular grooming will help keep your dog clean so that you can prevent some coat, skin, and health problems. Grooming should also be a special time between you and your Cocker. He can lie between your legs on the floor as you comb through his coat and check for tangles, burrs, and foxtails (grass seeds). Then you can give him a relaxing massage. This shouldn't be a chore, but instead can be used as bonding time.

Routine Care

Regular grooming sessions include baths, haircuts, and toenail trimming. But Cocker Spaniels need daily care in between these longer sessions. This is not an easy-care breed, but half an hour a day is usually sufficient.

Choose a time of day when you can spend this half hour with your dog with no interruptions. If you make a regular routine, it's much easier to stick to it rather than trying to fit in a half hour here one day and there another day. I like to do my grooming chores while watching television in the evening. I have my grooming tools, the dogs, and I turn on the news or a favorite program.

Brushing and Combing

Cocker Spaniels need to be brushed every day. It only takes one play session out in the wet grass or a dash through a field to cause tangles in that beautiful coat. And an ignored tangle of a few hairs will quickly turn into a mat (a huge tangle).

Get your pup started on grooming early, and he'll learn to accept and even enjoy it.

Plus, if you brush and comb the dog daily, it will only take a few minutes. If you ignore the coat for several days, it will be a much more difficult chore and neither you nor your dog will enjoy it.

To brush your Cocker, invite him to stand or lie down on the grooming table. (A grooming table is specifically made for grooming dogs. It's higher than most normal tables and has a nonskid surface on top. When you're not using it, it folds up.) If you don't have a grooming table, choose a table that is a good height for you (and your back) and put a rubber mat on it so your dog won't slip.

Separate a section of his coat with your hand and brush through it from the skin to the tips of the hair using the pin brush. If there are tangles, begin a few inches from the tips, brush that part, and gradually work up to the skin. When working on a tangle, hold the hair steady between the tangle and the skin so that you aren't pulling the hair and skin. If you pull, you will hurt your dog.

When the section of hair you are holding is brushed out, move on to another section. When the entire dog is brushed, go over him with a slicker brush to smooth everything out, and then a comb to find any last tangles and finish the job. Don't forget his legs, belly, and ears. These are among the places mats are likely to form.

Grooming Tools

Pin brush—a brush with straight metal bristles that have rounded tips

Slicker brush—a brush with many fine, bent metal pins

Comb—metal ones work best

Scissors—a six- or seven-inch straight pair

Conditioning shampoo

Drying agent—for the dog's ears

Cotton balls

Nail clippers

Clippers—electric or battery powered

Grooming table

If Your Dog Has a Mat

If you're combing and brushing your dog and you find a big tangle of hair, what do you do? First of all, using your fingers, see if you can pull the mat apart just as if you were untangling a knot in some string. If you can pull apart most of it, you may be able to comb out the rest.

If that doesn't work, use a bit of baby powder. Work it into the mat and then try to sort it out with your fingers or comb. Just as with tangles, make sure you hold the hair between the skin and the mat so that you don't pull on the hair and your dog's skin. If you pull, it will hurt and your dog will justifiably be upset.

Severe mats may need to be trimmed out of the coat. Be very careful doing this, because it's very easy to cut the dog's skin. Place your fingers between the mat and

Is there any doubt in your mind that this coat can tangle in an instant? Brush your dog regularly to avoid serious and painful coat problems.

your dog's skin. With the scissors held parallel to the dog's skin and your fingers, gently trim the mat, cutting just a few hairs at a time. Then comb it out of the coat and tell yourself that you will be more diligent with your combing so this won't happen again!

The Bath

I believe in frequent baths, especially for puppies. They get dirty so quickly. The old way of thinking was that frequent baths were too drying to the skin. In my experience, as long as you use a shampoo made specifically for dogs, this will not be a problem.

> **TIP**
>
> Before bathing your Cocker, it is important to comb out any mats. If you don't, the mats will get worse during the bath and will be even harder to deal with.

Young puppies can be bathed as often as every seven to fourteen days, but it is imperative you do this in a warm, draft-free environment. You must also thoroughly dry the puppy with towels and a hair dryer. Whether bathing a puppy or an adult, it is important that the dog is kept warm and thoroughly dried. Damp skin can result in hot spots—raw patches of itchy skin.

The most important thing to remember about bathing is not to get water in the dog's ears. You don't need to wet the top of the head or the top of the ears. These areas are seldom dirty and can be sponged off satisfactorily. Water in the ears promotes ear infections. You also need to be careful when using soap around your dog's eyes. Rinse them well with cold water if you think soap might have splashed into the eyes.

A good grooming or conditioning shampoo purchased from your veterinarian, groomer, or a pet supply shop will clean the average Cocker. There are many different types of shampoos available, especially for skin problems. Only your veterinarian should recommend a medicated shampoo. The different types control various problems, and you don't want to use them haphazardly; you could do damage to your dog's skin.

Last but not least, you need to clean out the dog's ears with a drying agent and cotton balls. Squirt in a few drops of a solution made with equal amounts of 3 percent hydrogen peroxide and 70 percent alcohol, or a commercial ear cleaning product, and wipe out the ears. This is very important after the bath, because you may have inadvertently gotten water into the dog's ears.

New Products in the Fight Against Fleas

At one time, battling fleas meant exposing your dog and yourself to toxic dips, sprays, powders, and collars. But today there are flea preventives that work very well and are safe for your dog, you, and the environment. The two most common types are insect growth regulators (IGRs), which stop the immature flea from developing or maturing, and adult flea killers. To deal with an active infestation, experts usually recommend a product that has both.

These next-generation flea fighters generally come in one of two forms:

- **Topical treatments or spot-ons.** These products are applied to the skin, usually between the shoulder blades. The product is absorbed through the skin into the dog's system.
- **Systemic products.** This is a pill your dog swallows that transmits a chemical throughout the dog's bloodstream. When a flea bites the dog, it picks up this chemical, which then prevents the flea's eggs from developing.

Talk to your veterinarian about which product is best for your dog. Make sure you read all the labels and apply the products exactly as recommended, and that you check to make sure they are safe for puppies.

Trimming Your Dog's Nails

Don't be afraid to trim your dog's nails. Most dogs are quite tolerant of having their nails trimmed, especially if you start them out slowly when they are young. Some dogs do fuss about it; these dogs must be properly restrained so they don't get away with their antics. If they do, they'll continually struggle until they get their way. Ask your veterinarian or the dog's breeder how to handle your dog if he fusses.

Unless your dog is black, you will probably find at least one light-colored nail on him. This will give you an idea of where the quick (the blood supply) stops.

Your veterinarian or a vet technician can show this to you. But if your dog has light nails, you can see it yourself—a white tip on the nail and then a solid pink section inside the nail. That solid section is the quick. If you cut into that, your dog will bleed. If you do cut a nail too short and cause it to bleed, sticking the nail in a soft piece of soap will stop the bleeding.

Nails should be trimmed weekly, but how much needs to be trimmed will vary. If your dog is active and regularly runs and plays, he may keep his nails worn down and may need just a tiny bit of trim. Other dogs may need a little more cut off. Nails that are not trimmed regularly can end up tearing. This is painful and means a trip to the veterinarian for treatment.

Trim your dog's nails weekly. Start out gently and he won't fuss.

Grooming Your Cocker Yourself

I talked about finding a professional groomer in chapter 5. But you can learn to groom your Cocker Spaniel yourself. Once a month should do it. Two advantages of doing this are that you can groom your dog more frequently and you can save money.

If you intend to do any grooming at home, a grooming table is helpful, although you can also use another table that places the dog at a height where you can work on him without bending over. Whatever type of table you use, it should be sturdy. If it wobbles, your dog will be frightened and uncooperative. Even if you plan to have your dog professionally groomed, a table comes in handy for the in-between combings. If you aren't using a grooming table, put a rubber mat on your table so your dog doesn't slide.

To groom your Cocker, you need a good set of electric or battery-powered pet clippers. These can be found at any pet supply store or department store with a good-size pet section. Many online stores sell them, as well.

Eventually you may want two or three different sizes of blades, but for now you should start with the #10, which is the most useful. Other blades include the #7F for trimming the back, the #40 for doing lip folds (the folds of skin around the dog's mouth) and the undersides of the ears, and the #15 for closer trimming of the face.

It is easiest to learn how to trim a Cocker if you are able to follow someone else's pattern. To do this, have your dog's breeder or groomer trim your Cocker, let his coat grow out for three or four weeks, then try it yourself. You will be able to see the hair that has grown out and identify what needs to be retrimmed. If you are afraid to try it, keep in mind that all your mistakes will grow out and you can do better the next time.

You'll need a good set of electric or battery-powered pet clippers if you want to groom your Cocker yourself.

The Trim

Every groomer and breeder has their own way of grooming a Cocker. As you work with your dog's coat, you'll find your own way, too, but here's one way to begin.

Start trimming with a #10 blade on the ear. Begin at the flap (which is about one-third of the way down), moving the clippers against the direction of growth of the hair up to the top of the ear and lifting the clippers a little where the ear meets the skull. This is so you don't dig into that area and create a ridge. Next, hold the ear up and clip the underside, trimming very close around the opening.

> **TIP**
>
> Not all coat trimmings need to end with a bath. Trimmings in between baths are fine. I prefer to trim before bathing so I can trim any loose ends after the dog is dry.

Then begin trimming the muzzle and sides of the head, paying particular attention to the lip fold areas (all the folds around the dog's mouth and muzzle) and the corners of the eyes. These areas need to be trimmed as close as possible, so hold the dog's head steady as you work. Trim the top of the head by moving the clippers with the direction of growth of the hair.

Every groomer has their own style for trimming the ears. Find what works for you and your dog.

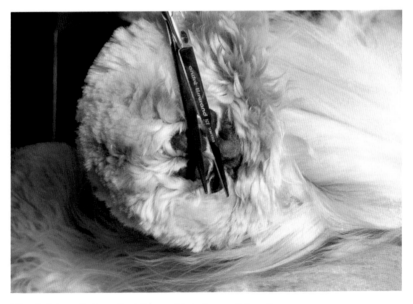

Trim the hair on the feet so that it is even with the bottom of the pads.

Do the front of the neck next, using the clippers against the direction of growth of the hair. Next, take the clippers, going with the hair, down the side of the neck, trying to blend it in.

You would never use a clipper on the back of a show dog, but it's routinely done on pets. The #7 blade is better, leaving the coat a little longer than the #10. Clip carefully along the back and a small way down the sides, going with the direction of the hair. The dog's tail can be cleaned up with the scissors. Trim all the loose hairs so the tail looks neat.

The legs can be a challenge. Most groomers clip the elbow and around it with a #10 blade. This area mats easily, so it's a good idea to clip it to prevent mats from forming. You need to comb the legs as you're working. They can be scissored short (about two inches) for a pet cut (also called a puppy cut) or they can be left long.

Cockers shown in dog shows are currently being trimmed so their hair doesn't drag on the floor. Start at the foot, shaping the hair on it with straight scissors and trimming away hair under the feet so it's even with the bottom of the pads. After the feet are done, you can layer the feathering on the legs, shortening the hair, starting at the foot. This isn't necessary, but if you feel creative you may want to give it a try.

External Parasites

External parasites live on the outside of your dog's body. Unfortunately, they can cause your dog great discomfort, irritation, and illness. It's very important that you make sure parasites stay off him.

Fleas

A flea is a crescent-shaped insect, about the size of the head of a pin, with six legs. It is a tremendous jumper. Fleas live by biting a host animal and drinking its blood.

You can see fleas by brushing the dog's coat against the lie of the hair and looking at the skin. A flea will appear as a tiny darting speck, trying to hide in the hair.

Nasty parasites can lurk in even the nicest backyards. Make sure your dog is protected.

Making Your Environment Flea Free

If there are fleas on your dog, there are fleas in your home, yard, and car, even if you can't see them. Take these steps to combat them.

In your home:
- Wash whatever is washable (the dog bed, sheets, blankets, pillow covers, slipcovers, curtains, etc.).
- Vacuum everything else in your home—furniture, floors, rugs, everything. Pay special attention to the folds and crevices in upholstery, the cracks between floorboards, and the spaces between the floor and the baseboards. Flea larvae are sensitive to sunlight, so inside the house they prefer deep carpet, bedding, and cracks and crevices.
- When you're done, throw the vacuum cleaner bag away—in an outside garbage can.
- Use a nontoxic flea-killing powder to treat your carpets (but remember, it does not control fleas elsewhere in the house). The powder stays deep in the carpet and kills fleas (using a form of boric acid) for up to a year.
- If you have a particularly serious flea problem, consider using a fogger or long-lasting spray to kill any adult and larval fleas, or having a professional exterminator treat your home.

Fleas show up best on the dog's belly, near the genitals. You can also look for them by having your dog lie on a solid-colored sheet and brushing vigorously. If you see salt-and-pepper–type residue falling to the sheet, your Cocker has fleas. The residue is made up of fecal matter (the "pepper") and eggs (the "salt").

Fleas biting their host can also cause other problems. Many dogs are allergic to the flea's saliva and scratch each bite until a sore develops. This is called flea allergy dermatitis, and is a serious problem in many areas of the country. Fleas can also carry disease, such as plague, and are the intermediary host for tapeworms, an internal parasite.

To reduce the flea population, you need to treat the dog and his environment (see the box above). If you treat only the dog and do not treat the house, yard,

In your car:

- Take out the floor mats and hose them down with a strong stream of water, then hang them up to dry in the sun.
- Wash any towels, blankets, or other bedding you regularly keep in the car.
- Thoroughly vacuum the entire interior of your car, paying special attention to the seams between the bottom and back of the seats.
- When you're done, throw the vacuum cleaner bag away—in an outside garbage can.

In your yard:

- Flea larvae prefer shaded areas that have plenty of organic material and moisture, so rake the yard thoroughly and bag all the debris in tightly sealed bags.
- Spray your yard with an insecticide that has residual activity for at least thirty days. Insecticides that use a form of boric acid are nontoxic. Some products contain an insect growth regulator (such as fenoxycarb) and need to be applied only once or twice a year.
- For an especially difficult flea problem, consider having an exterminator treat your yard.
- Keep your yard free of piles of leaves, weeds, and other organic debris. Be especially careful in shady, moist areas, such as under bushes.

and car, your dog will simply become reinfested. Flea eggs can live in the environment for years, waiting for the right conditions to hatch. This is not an insect that can be ignored!

Ticks

As you examine your dog for fleas, also check for ticks that may have lodged in the ears or in the hair at the base of the ear, the armpits, or around the genitals. If you find a tick, remove it as described in the box on page 74. Don't just grab and pull or the tick's head may separate from the body. If the head remains in the skin, an infection or abscess may result and veterinary treatment may be required.

How to Get Rid of a Tick

Although many of the new generation of flea fighters are partially effective in killing ticks once they are on your dog, they are not 100 percent effective and will not keep ticks from biting your dog in the first place. During tick season (which, depending on where you live, can be spring, summer, and/or fall), examine your dog every day for ticks. Pay particular attention to your dog's neck, behind the ears, the armpits, and the groin.

When you find a tick, use a pair of tweezers to grasp the tick as close as possible to the dog's skin and pull it out using firm, steady pressure. Check to make sure you get the whole tick (mouth parts left in your dog's skin can cause an infection), then wash the wound and dab it with a little antibiotic ointment. Watch for signs of inflammation.

Ticks carry very serious diseases that are transmittable to humans, so dispose of the tick safely. *Never* crush it between your fingers. Don't flush it down the toilet either, because the tick will survive the trip and infect another animal. Instead, use the tweezers to place the tick in a tight-sealing jar or plastic dish with a little alcohol, put on the lid, and dispose of the container in an outdoor garbage can. Wash the tweezers thoroughly with hot water and alcohol.

Chapter 8

Keeping Your Cocker Spaniel Healthy

Cocker Spaniels are, for the most part, healthy, hearty dogs. However, like all dog breeds, they can have some health challenges. If you know about these problems, you can protect your dog from them and know what to do if a health issue does arise. Keep in mind, too, that your dog's veterinarian is an important partner in your dog's continued good health.

Health Problems Seen in Cockers

Although Cockers are generally quite healthy, every breed, including the Cocker Spaniel, has some health problems that are more commonly seen in that particular breed. They are listed here so that you can be aware of them and get your dog veterinary help if it is needed. It certainly does not mean that your dog will develop one or all of these problems; often that is determined by your dog's genetic heritage.

Allergies

Allergies can range in scope from mildly annoying to very serious. Mildly annoying may result in watery eyes or some sneezing, while very serious allergies can cause severe skin problems, ear infections, and even anaphylactic shock. Cockers may be allergic to food ingredients, specific vaccinations, mold or mildew, pollen, or a host of other substances. If you believe your dog may be suffering from allergies, talk to your veterinarian. Allergies tests may be recommended.

Your veterinarian is your partner in maintaining your dog's health.

Anal Sac Problems

The anal sacs are located under the skin on either side of the anus. They should normally empty when the dog has a bowel movement. If they do not, they may cause the dog discomfort when they are full. Symptoms of impacted glands and possible inflammation are excessive licking under the tail and/or bloody or sticky discharge from the anal area. Your dog may also scoot her rear along the floor. Veterinary attention is required. Many veterinarians do not recommend emptying the sacs unless there are symptoms of a problem, because the glands could become habitually irritated.

Autoimmune Diseases

Two autoimmune diseases have been seen in Cockers: autoimmune hemolytic anemia (a blood cell disease) and autoimmune thyroiditis (a thyroid disease). With both diseases, the dog's immune system begins attacking its own cells, causing severe health problems. In most cases, treatment will help.

Colitis

This is an intermittent inflammation of the colon. The dog's stool may be very soft, runny, and may have blood in it. Colitis could be the result of undiagnosed whipworms or other internal parasites, an unfamiliar food, or no explainable reason. Frequently the dog feels fine and is willing to eat. At-home treatment could consist of Pepto-Bismol (given according to the dog's weight—talk to your veterinarian about the dose), withholding food for twenty-four hours and then reintroducing small amounts of food. If the condition persists, if there is blood in the stool, or if the dog is acting poorly, seek professional help.

Ear Problems

Cocker Spaniels are well known for their ear problems, which many people attribute to their long, pendulous ears (they certainly don't help). Allergies can add to ear problems, as can several other health problems.

Ear Infection

This is an inflammation of the external ear canal that begins at the outside opening of the ear and extends inward to the eardrum.

Preventing ear infections is most important, especially if your dog is prone to them. Keep the insides of the ears dry. If the dog goes swimming or is outside playing in the rain, gently dry the inside of the ears. Clean the ears frequently with a commercial product made for this purpose or with a cleaning solution recommended by your veterinarian.

Ear Margin Seborrhea

The ear margins (the edges of the ears) may have small, greasy plugs adhering to the skin. This is common in some dogs with pendulous ears, and may be a permanent problem. You can remove the accumulated material with your thumbnail and wash the areas with dandruff shampoo twice a week (ask your vet which shampoo to use). I have found using a snood on the dog during feeding decreases the problem (a snood is a cloth wrap that acts like a headband to keep a dog's ears from falling into her food or water).

Eye Problems

This breed may be prone to several eye defects, including cataracts (cloudiness in the lens of the eye), progressive retinal atrophy (a defect of the retina that causes blindness), retinal dysplasia (folds in the retina), and glaucoma (increased pressure in the eye).

If you see your dog squinting, rubbing her eyes, or otherwise bothered by her eyes, get her in to your veterinarian right away.

Blocked Tear Ducts

Cocker Spaniels are prone to blocked tear ducts, which may or may not need to be opened by a veterinarian. A blocked tear duct may cause eye irritation, dry eyes, or even excessive tearing. If your dog rubs her face along the carpet, paws at her eyes, squints, or has excessive tearing, get her to the veterinarian to have her eyes checked.

Cherry Eye

In a dog with cherry eye, you may notice a red, cherry-like gland showing in the corner of the eye. An infected tear gland on the surface of the third eyelid causes this condition. Although it looks horrible, this is not a medical emergency. But you should take the dog to the veterinarian as soon as possible.

Because of their loose lower eyelids, Cocker Spaniels are prone to a few eye problems.

Frequently, the vet can push the gland back to its normal place. Then, treated with an ophthalmic, antibiotic, steroid ointment, it may regress. Even if the cherry eye regresses, it may reappear days, weeks, or months later.

Conjunctivitis

The conjunctiva is the pink tissue that lines the inner surface of the eyelids and covers the front portions of the eyeball (except the clear, transparent cornea). The conjunctiva may become red, swollen, and damaged by irritating substances such as bacteria, foreign matter, or chemicals. Allergies may also be the culprit. You should see your veterinarian for diagnosis and treatment.

It is important to keep the hair trimmed short around the eyes. Long hair stays damp and contributes to the problem. Clean the dog's eyes every day with warm water and wipe away any matter that has accumulated in the corners.

Dry Eye

This is a disease in which tear production is absent or decreased. The cornea dries out and becomes painful. Untreated, dry eye can result in loss of vision.

Unfortunately, this is a common problem in Cockers. It may be immune-mediated, although experts feel there may be many potential causes. Sometimes a white-gray discharge can be found around the eye. The eye itself may be yellow if the condition has persisted for a while. If you do see this, have your dog's tear production checked. I have found tear production can vary, so you may need to check it more than once. Fortunately, a drug is available that effectively keeps this condition under control.

Flea Allergy Dermatitis

This is caused by hypersensitivity (allergy) to flea saliva. The bite of one flea can cause the dog to bite, lick, and scratch herself raw. Your dog may need medical attention. You should immediately treat your dog and her environment for fleas (as described in chapter 7). Trim and wash the involved area on your dog—daily if it is oozing—and treat with an antibiotic, anti-inflammatory skin product. These inflamed areas are commonly called hot spots.

Hip Dysplasia

Hip dysplasia is a failure of the head of the femur (thighbone) to fit properly into the acetabulum (hip socket). The resulting laxness in the hip joint can vary from mildly annoying to the dog to crippling. It cannot be diagnosed by watching a dog walk; X-rays are necessary. Your veterinarian can help you decide on the appropriate treatment.

Structural abnormalities such as hip dysplasia can prevent a dog from enjoying an active lifestyle.

Vaccines

What vaccines dogs need and how often they need them has been a subject of controversy for several years. Researchers, health care professionals, vaccine manufacturers, and dog owners do not always agree on which vaccines each dog needs or how often booster shots must be given.

In 2006, the American Animal Hospital Association issued a set of vaccination guidelines and recommendations intended to help dog owners and veterinarians sort through much of the controversy and conflicting information. The guidelines designate four vaccines as core, or essential for every dog, because of the serious nature of the diseases and their widespread distribution. These are canine distemper virus (using a modified live virus or recombinant modified live virus vaccine), canine parvovirus (using a modified live virus vaccine), canine adenovirus-2 (using a modified live virus vaccine), and rabies (using a killed virus). The general recommendations for their administration (except rabies, for which you must follow local laws) are:

- Vaccinate puppies at 6–8 weeks, 9–11 weeks, and 12–14 weeks.
- Give an initial "adult" vaccination when the dog is older than 16 weeks; two doses, three to four weeks apart, are advised, but one dose is considered protective and acceptable.

Interdigital Cysts

These are small swellings between the toes, usually associated with a staphylococcus (bacterial) infection. A home remedy is to soak the affected foot in a couple of quarts of warm water with a cup of Epsom salts dissolved in it, twice a day for two to three days. Make sure you dry the foot after the soak. If the cysts become a recurring problem, take your dog to your veterinarian.

- Give a booster shot when the dog is 1 year old.
- Give a subsequent booster shot every three years, unless there are risk factors that make it necessary to vaccinate more or less often.

Noncore vaccines should only be considered for those dogs who risk exposure to a particular disease because of geographic area, lifestyle, frequency of travel, or other issues. They include vaccines against distemper-measles virus, canine parainfluenza virus, leptospirosis, *Bordetella bronchiseptica*, and *Borrelia burgdorferi* (Lyme disease).

Vaccines that are not generally recommended because the disease poses little risk to dogs or is easily treatable, or the vaccine has not been proven to be effective, are those against giardia, canine coronavirus, and canine adenovirus-1.

Often, combination injections are given to puppies, with one shot containing several core and noncore vaccines. Your veterinarian may be reluctant to use separate shots that do not include the noncore vaccines, because they must be specially ordered. If you are concerned about these noncore vaccines, talk to your vet.

Lip Fold Pyoderma

Dogs who salivate excessively are at the greatest risk to develop bacterial inflammations in the lip folds and creases. The best prevention is to keep the hair cut short along the lip folds. Depending on the dog, trimming may need to be done weekly. Wash the inflamed area with an iodine scrub once a day, or more frequently depending on the severity. Use baby powder in the folds to help keep them dry.

Luxating Patella

The patella is the kneecap. In a dog with luxating patella, the kneecap will slip, causing the dog to lift that leg and skip a step. Many dogs learn to lift the leg, stretch it out behind them (thereby realigning the knee), and then continue on their way. This is not an emergency, but should be checked by a veterinarian because it can progressively get worse.

Seizure Disorders

Many breeds suffer from seizure disorders, including epilepsy, and unfortunately this has been seen in Cocker Spaniels, too. If your dog suffers from any kind of a seizure, from mild tremors to a full convulsion, get her in to her veterinarian as soon as you can move her. Seizures can be caused by many different things and many can be life-threatening.

Thyroid Disease

Cockers can develop an autoimmune disease that attacks the thyroid gland. They have also been known to be diagnosed with hypothyroidism. This occurs when the thyroid gland does not produce enough of the thyroid hormone for the body to function correctly. Symptoms include a slowed metabolism and

Lethargy and unexplained weight gain are two signs of hypothyroidism. Take your dog to the veterinarian if you see any change in what is normal for your dog.

weight gain, hair loss, and a darkening of the skin. Treatment is available so the dog can live a normal life.

Vaccine Reactions

Cocker Spaniels are one of the breeds known to have allergic reactions to several commonly given vaccinations. Cockers have been known to develop immune system problems after vaccinations, especially repeated vaccines. It is very important to discuss potential problems with your veterinarian and to have your vet check your dog's blood antibodies for specific diseases before giving booster shots. If your dog has sufficient antibodies, booster shots may not be needed.

Von Willebrand's Disease

In dogs with this disease, the blood does not clot normally and even a bruise can become a problem. This is often first diagnosed when the dog goes in to be spayed or neutered and has a bleeding problem during surgery. The puppy may also bleed more than normally when losing her puppy teeth and growing in adult teeth. If you notice any unusual bleeding or bruising, get your dog in to the veterinarian right away.

Know Your Dog's Normal

Every pet owner should recognize what is normal for their dog. You should always pay attention to your dog's eating and elimination habits as well. And watch the way she moves. That way, you will be the first to notice a change in your dog's appearance or behavior.

Being able to take your dog's temperature and check her gums and heart rate are important steps toward making sure your dog is as healthy as possible. Once a month, give your dog a quick home checkup, too.

> **TIP**
>
> With careful observation and routine physicals by the veterinarian, you will greatly enhance your dogs' life.

Taking Your Dog's Temperature

A dog's normal temperature is 100.5 to 102.5 degrees Fahrenheit. Use a rectal thermometer. With your dog standing, shake down the thermometer, then lubricate the end with some petroleum jelly. Insert the thermometer approximately one inch into the rectum (less on a young puppy). Keep one hand under your dog's tummy so she doesn't sit down, and use the other hand to hold on to the end of the thermometer. Take it out to read after one minute. (New digital thermometers may be even quicker.)

Checking Gum Color

Correct gum color is very important. Check it periodically when your dog is in good health so you can recognize anything abnormal—a sure sign that your dog is not feeling well. There may be black pigmentation around the gums, but in general they should be bright pink, like yours. There should never be any yellowish tint to the gums. Pale gums suggest shock or anemia and are definitely signs of an emergency.

If you suspect a problem, press your thumb against the gum, which will whiten the spot. When you remove your thumb, check how long it takes for the spot to turn pink again. Normal capillary refill time (the time it takes for the pink color to return) is one to two seconds.

Heart Rate and Pulse

The heart rate in healthy Cockers is usually around 100 to 120 beats per minute. The exact heart rate in a healthy dog depends on her size and condition. It is faster in small dogs and puppies and slower in large dogs or those in good physical condition.

You can feel your dog's pulse by placing your fingers against the dog's chest just below her elbow. Count the number of beats in a minute. You can also measure your dog's pulse by placing your fingers on her femoral artery, located in the groin area. Find the artery by feeling along the inner thigh where the leg and body meet.

Get in the habit of checking your dog's eyes. Gently wipe away any matter that has gathered in the corners.

Eye Exam

Cockers have beautiful eyes. Therefore, it should be easy to notice anything out of the ordinary in them. Check the cornea (the clear part of the eye). Is it bright and shiny? Are the pupils of equal size? Do they constrict in response to light? Are the pupils black, or is there a gray-blue haziness or white cloudiness in them? Many old dogs have a blue haziness in their pupils, which may be a normal aging change. You should confirm any changes with your veterinarian.

Is the third eyelid partially protruding over the eye? Is there discharge or evidence of tearing? Is the white of the eye reddened or discolored? The white of the eye should never appear yellowish. Are the pink mucous membranes that surround the eye (the conjunctiva) pale, normal, or irritated?

Anything out of the ordinary or any changes should be brought to your veterinarian's attention.

Ear Exam

Check your dog's ears daily. Do the ears have an odor? Healthy ears smell damp but not bad. Infected ears have a sour or yeasty smell. Are they clean or dirty? Is your dog shaking her head or scratching her ears a lot? Does the dog seem to have pain in or around her ears? Dirty ears should be washed, but painful or inflamed ears should be seen by your veterinarian. The vet needs to see the problem, so don't wash them before the veterinary visit.

Mouth Exam

Check your dog's mouth and get her used to you handling it. Is there brown or yellow buildup (calculus) around the teeth? Calculus can cause the gums to

Keep your dog's ears dry and check them daily. Clean them if they're dirty.

When to Call the Veterinarian

Go to the vet right away or take your dog to an emergency veterinary clinic if:

- Your dog is choking
- Your dog is having trouble breathing
- Your dog has been injured and you cannot stop the bleeding within a few minutes
- Your dog has been stung or bitten by an insect and the site is swelling
- Your dog has been bitten by a snake
- Your dog has been bitten by another animal (including a dog) and shows any swelling or bleeding
- Your dog has touched, licked, or in any way been exposed to poison
- Your dog has been burned by either heat or caustic chemicals
- Your dog has been hit by a car
- Your dog has any obvious broken bones or cannot put any weight on one of her limbs
- Your dog has a seizure

Make an appointment to see the vet as soon as possible if:

- Your dog has been bitten by a cat, another dog, or a wild animal
- Your dog has been injured and is still limping an hour later

recede, which results in premature loosening of the teeth (periodontal disease). Inflammation and redness around the gums (gingivitis) usually accompanies the presence of calculus. Are there any tumors inside or outside the mouth? Check the lip folds for inflammation.

Skin and Coat

Is the coat shiny or dry and brittle? Are there areas of thinning hair or hair loss? Does your dog have an itching problem? Can you see skin lesions or red, inflamed areas? How about fleas and ticks? Is there an abnormal odor to the

- Your dog has unexplained swelling or redness
- Your dog's appetite changes
- Your dog vomits repeatedly and can't seem to keep food down, or drools excessively while eating
- You see any changes in your dog's urination or defecation (pain during elimination, change in regular habits, blood in urine or stool, diarrhea, foul-smelling stool)
- Your dog scoots her rear end on the floor
- Your dog's energy level, attitude, or behavior changes for no apparent reason
- Your dog has crusty or cloudy eyes, or excessive tearing or discharge
- Your dog's nose is dry or chapped, hot, crusty, or runny
- Your dog's ears smell foul, have a dark discharge, or seem excessively waxy
- Your dog's gums are inflamed or bleeding, her teeth look brown, or her breath is foul
- Your dog's skin is red, flaky, itchy, or inflamed, or she keeps chewing at certain spots
- Your dog's coat is dull, dry, brittle, or bare in spots
- Your dog's paws are red, swollen, tender, cracked, or the nails are split or too long
- Your dog is panting excessively, wheezing, unable to catch her breath, breathing heavily, or sounds strange when she breathes

skin? Any irritations or swellings between the toes? These are all conditions to look for. If you see them, take your dog to the veterinarian.

Check the Nose

A healthy dog's nose is usually cool and moist. However, the temperature or wetness of the dog's nose is not necessarily an indication of her health. A sick dog may have a warm, dry nose or a cool, wet one. Look for other signs if you suspect a health problem. Any secretion from the nose should be clear and watery, not thick, cloudy, or colored.

Why Spay and Neuter?

Breeding dogs is a serious undertaking that should only be part of a well-planned breeding program. Why? Because dogs pass on their physical and behavioral problems to their offspring. Even healthy, well-behaved dogs can pass on problems in their genes.

Is your dog so sweet that you'd like to have a litter of puppies just like her? If you breed her to another dog, the pups will not have the same genetic heritage she has. Breeding her *parents* again will increase the odds of a similar pup, but even then, the puppies in the second litter could inherit different genes. In fact, *there is no way to breed a dog to be just like another dog.*

Meanwhile, thousands and thousands of dogs are killed in animal shelters every year simply because they have no homes. Casual breeding is a big contributor to this problem.

If you don't plan to breed your dog, is it still a good idea to spay her or neuter him? Yes!

When you spay your female:

- You avoid her heat cycles, during which she discharges blood and scent.
- It greatly reduces the risk of mammary cancer and eliminates the risk of pyometra (an often fatal infection of the uterus) and uterine cancer.
- It prevents unwanted pregnancies.
- It reduces dominance behaviors and aggression.

When you neuter your male:

- It curbs the desire to roam and to fight with other males.
- It greatly reduces the risk of prostate cancer and eliminates the risk of testicular cancer.
- It helps reduce leg lifting and mounting behavior.
- It reduces dominance behaviors and aggression.

Urinary and Reproductive System Health

Is your dog drinking and urinating frequently? Does she urinate a normal amount or small amounts more frequently? Does she strain while urinating? Is there blood in the urine?

Check your female for any vaginal discharge. Has she been licking herself a lot? Vaginitis is quite common in female puppies before their first heat cycle. Check your female's mammary glands (breasts and nipples). Examine each one carefully for any bumps. Report anything unusual to your veterinarian immediately.

Examination of the male's reproductive system starts at the penis. A small amount of thick, greenish discharge may be present in adult unneutered males, but is not usually present in neutered males. This discharge should be washed off and treated by your veterinarian if it persists. Excessive licking or irritation of the prepuce (front of the penile shaft) results in redness or pain upon examination. If your dog is not neutered, examine his scrotum. Is the skin irritated, thickened, or discolored? Palpate each testicle. Are they symmetric and uniform in size and shape? Is there any pain on examination of the scrotum or testes? Again, report anything unusual immediately.

Internal Parasites

Parasites such as fleas and ticks that live on the outside of your Cocker's body were discussed in chapter 7. With internal parasites, you can't see the problem and you may not even see any signs of an infestation until it has progressed. That's yet another reason why regular checkups are so important.

Ascarids (Roundworms)

These long, white worms are common, especially in puppies, although they occasionally infest adult dogs and even people. The adult female roundworm can lay up to 200,000 eggs a day, which are passed in the dog's feces. Roundworms are transmitted only via the feces. Because of this, stools should be picked up daily and your dog should be prevented from investigating other dogs' feces.

If treated early, roundworms are not serious. However, a heavy infestation can severely affect a dog's health. Puppies with roundworms will not thrive and will appear thin, with a dull coat and a pot belly.

In people, roundworms can be more serious. Therefore, early treatment, regular fecal checks, and good sanitation are important, both for your Cocker's continued good health and yours.

Internal parasites are a bigger danger to puppies, who become infested more easily than adults and tend to be sicker when they are.

Giardia

This protozoal disease infects mammals and birds. The parasites live in the small intestines and are acquired when cysts are ingested from contaminated water.

Giardia is common in wild animals in many areas, so be careful if you take your Cocker walking in the wilderness. If she drinks out of the local spring or stream, she can pick up giardia—just as you can. Diarrhea is one of the first signs. If your dog has diarrhea and you and your dog have been out in the wilds, make sure you tell your veterinarian.

Heartworms

Adult heartworms live in the upper heart and greater pulmonary arteries, where they damage the vessel walls. Poor circulation results, which damages other bodily functions, eventually causing death from heart failure.

The adult worms produce thousands of tiny larvae called microfilaria. These circulate throughout the bloodstream until they are sucked up by an intermediate host, a mosquito. The microfilaria go through the larval stages in the mosquito, then are transferred back to another dog when the mosquito bites again.

Dogs infected with heartworms can be treated if caught early. Unfortunately, the treatment itself can be risky and has killed some dogs. However, preventive medications are available that kill the larvae. Heartworm can be diagnosed by a blood test, and a negative result is required before starting the preventive meds.

Hookworms

Hookworms live their adult lives in the small intestines of dogs and other animals. They attach to the intestinal wall and suck blood. When they detach and move to a new location, the old wound continues to bleed because of the anticoagulant the worm injects when it bites. Because of this, bloody diarrhea is usually the first sign of a problem.

Hookworm eggs are passed through the feces. Either they are picked up from the stools, as with roundworms, or, if conditions are right, they hatch in the soil and attach themselves to the feet of their new hosts, where they can burrow

Heartworms live any place where there are mosquitoes. Preventing them is much easier and safer than treating an infestation.

through the skin. They then migrate to the intestinal tract, where the cycle starts all over again.

People can pick up hookworms by walking barefoot in infected soil. In the Sunbelt states, children often pick up hookworm eggs when playing outside in the dirt or in a sandbox. Treatment, for both dogs and people, may have to be repeated.

Tapeworms

Tapeworms attach to the intestinal wall to absorb nutrients. They grow by creating new segments, and usually the first signs of an infestation are the ricelike segments found in the stools or on the dog's coat near the rectum. Tapeworms are acquired when the dog chews at a flea bite and swallows a flea, which is the intermediate host. Therefore, a good flea-control program is the best way to prevent a tapeworm infestation.

Whipworms

Adult whipworms live in the large intestines, where they feed on blood. The eggs are passed in the stool and can live in the soil for many years. If your dog eats the fresh spring grass or buries her bone in the yard, she can pick up whipworm eggs from the infected soil. If you garden, you can pick up eggs under your fingernails, infecting yourself if you touch your face.

Heavy infestations cause diarrhea, often watery or bloody. The dog may appear thin and anemic, with a poor coat. Severe bowel problems may result. Unfortunately, whipworms can be difficult to detect because the worms do not continually shed eggs. Therefore, a stool sample may be clear one day and show eggs the next.

Emergency Care

Make it a point to familiarize yourself with your veterinarian: Keep his or her phone number by the telephone; know his or her policy for after-hours care; find out where the emergency clinic is and go there when it's not an emergency so you'll be prepared when one arises. *If you have a real emergency, time is of the essence.* The more familiar you are with all aspects of emergency care, the better chance you'll have of possibly saving your dog's life.

Anything that is potentially life threatening or causes a great deal of pain or distress for your dog is an emergency. The box on pages 86–87 lists many emergency situations that require immediate veterinary care. In addition, pale gums and an abnormal heart rate could indicate that your dog is in shock, which is an emergency. And spinal paralysis needs to be treated within a few hours of onset. Spinal problems need to be handled very carefully, with dogs kept confined and quiet until they get to the vet.

The rest of the conditions discussed below range from mild to serious. Read about them now so you'll have a better idea of how to handle them if they happen to your dog.

Antifreeze Poisoning

Antifreeze is a quick killer. Dogs like it because it is sweet, and they'll be attracted to any spills in your garage or driveway. This is an emergency and your dog needs *immediate* treatment. Nonpoisonous types of anti-freeze are now available. They are more expensive than the toxic brands, but that's a small price to pay for your dog's safety.

Bee Stings

Bee stings can become an emergency if your dog is stung several times or has an allergic reaction. Symptoms include swelling around the muzzle and face. Check the gum color immediately; the gums should look pink and healthy. Very pale gums are signs of a problem. Monitor swelling, keep checking gum color, and pay attention to your dog's breathing. A severe reaction can cause difficulty in breathing, collapse, and sometimes, death.

Bites

If your dog is bitten by another dog or animal, wash the area thoroughly. Your dog may need to have the wound professionally cleaned and possibly stitched. If your dog was bitten by another dog, find out if that dog is well vaccinated, including being up to date on rabies vaccine. If your dog was bitten by a wild animal or a stray dog, make sure you tell your veterinarian that so your dog's vaccination records can be checked.

Bleeding

Apply a clean bandage to a wound, wrapping it tightly enough to prevent blood from dripping through but not so tight as to stop the circulation. Gauze is better than cotton, because cotton will stick to

Cockers can get bitten or stung by insects even through that full coat.

the wound. If a regular bandage is not immediately available, a small towel or clean washcloth can serve as a bandage, secured with a stocking, scarf, or necktie. Anything more serious than a scrape or small cut (both of which should be washed and dressed with antibiotic ointment) requires a visit to the veterinarian.

Burns

Rinse a burn with cool water right away. Burns cause pain and even shock if they are large or serious. Call your veterinarian immediately; burns can be very debilitating. With proper care, the skin should slough off in about three weeks. If the burn is severe, hair loss could be permanent.

Chocolate Toxicosis

Ten ounces of milk chocolate (a large candy bar) can kill a twelve-pound dog. Chocolate toxicosis is a common problem because dogs like chocolate almost as much as people do. Caffeine and theobromine, two chemicals in chocolate, can damage a dog's nervous system. Symptoms of chocolate toxicosis may include restlessness, vomiting, increased heart rate, seizure, or coma. Get veterinary help right away.

How to Make a Canine First-Aid Kit

If your dog hurts herself, even a minor cut, it can be very upsetting for both of you. Having a first-aid kit handy will help you to help her, calmly and efficiently. What should be in your canine first-aid kit?

- Antibiotic ointment
- Antiseptic and antibacterial cleansing wipes
- Benadryl
- Cotton-tipped applicators
- Disposable razor
- Elastic wrap bandages
- Extra leash and collar
- First-aid tape of various widths
- Gauze bandage roll
- Gauze pads of different sizes, including eye pads
- Hydrogen peroxide
- Instant cold compress
- Kaopectate or Pepto-Bismol tablets or liquid
- Latex gloves
- Lubricating jelly
- Muzzle
- Nail clippers
- Pen, pencil, and paper for notes and directions
- Plastic syringe with no needle (for administering liquids)
- Round-ended scissors and pointy scissors
- Safety pins
- Sterile saline eyewash
- Thermometer (rectal)
- Tweezers

Choking

If you notice that your dog is choking, open her mouth wide to see if any object is visible. Try to remove the object. Extend her neck and pull her tongue forward to help remove anything. If you don't see anything but she's still choking, lay her on her side and apply abdominal thrusts by squeezing sharply just below the ribs. Call your veterinarian immediately.

Drowning

Remove any debris your dog may have swallowed, and then hold her upside down. Swing her gently a few times so that water can drain from her mouth and lungs. Pull the tongue forward to stimulate breathing. Call your veterinarian. If the dog has been in cold water, wrap her in blankets.

Electrocution

If you see your dog being electrocuted, by chewing on an electric cord, for example, *turn off the current before touching her.* Try to resuscitate your dog by pulling the tongue forward to stimulate breathing. If your dog isn't breathing, try mouth-to-muzzle breathing. Don't give up, and call the vet right away.

Heatstroke

Classic signs of heatstroke are rapid, shallow breathing, rapid heartbeat, a temperature above 104 degrees Fahrenheit, and subsequent collapse. It's important to cool your dog off as quickly as possible. Spray or sponge her down with cool water and pack ice around the head, neck, and groin. Monitor the dog's temperature and stop the cooling process when it reaches 103 degrees. Continue to monitor the temperature to be sure it doesn't go back up. In any case, get veterinary attention immediately.

Your dog relies on you to stay calm and do the right thing in an emergency.

A dog with so much coat can rapidly get overheated. Heatstroke is an emergency and requires immediate treatment.

ASPCA Animal Poison Control Center

The ASPCA Animal Poison Control Center has a staff of licensed veterinarians and board-certified toxicologists available 24 hours a day, 365 days a year. The number to call is (888) 426-4435. You will be charged a consultation fee of $60 per case, charged to most major credit cards. There is no charge for follow-up calls in critical cases. At your request, they will also contact your veterinarian. Specific treatment and information can be provided via fax.

Keep the poison control number in large, legible print with your other emergency telephone numbers. When you call, be prepared to give your name, address, and phone number; what your dog has gotten into (the amount and how long ago); your dog's breed, age, sex, and weight; and what signs and symptoms the dog is showing. You can log onto www.aspca.org and click on "Animal Poison Control Center" for more information, including a list of toxic and nontoxic plants.

Poisoning

A dog can be poisoned by numerous things, including toxins in garbage. Various poisons are treated differently, so it's not always wise to induce vomiting. Symptoms of poisoning include muscle trembling and weakness, increased salivation, vomiting, and loss of bowel control.

Call your veterinarian immediately if you suspect poisoning. Knowing the source will help your vet immensely. Keep the numbers of a local poison control center (if you have one) and the national poison control center by the phone.

Seizures

Generally, a small seizure is not considered an emergency. However, you should notify your veterinarian as soon as the seizure is over because many health problems can cause a seizure. Cockers (as well as other breeds) may be predisposed to seizures. Dogs do not swallow their tongues during a seizure. However, handling the mouth should be avoided, because you may be accidentally bitten. Loss of consciousness, defecating, or urinating may or may not occur. Keep your dog in a safe place so she doesn't fall off furniture or down the stairs, or bang her head into anything.

Shock

Shock is life-threatening and demands immediate veterinary care. It can occur after injury or even after a serious fright. Other causes are hemorrhage, fluid loss, poisoning, or collapse of a body system.

Symptoms of shock are a rapid and weak pulse, shallow breathing, dilated pupils, subnormal temperature, and muscle weakness. Capillary refill time is slow. Keep your dog warm while taking her immediately to the vet.

Skunk Spray

Being sprayed by a skunk is not really a life-threatening emergency—but it would be in my house! The old remedy is to wash the dog in tomato juice, followed by a soap and water bath. You can also try bathing the dog in a mixture that consists of one quart 3 percent hydrogen peroxide, one-quarter cup baking soda, and one teaspoon liquid soap. Or you can try one of the new deskunking formulas available at pet supply stores.

A dog who has been skunked is not welcome in my house! She needs to be washed in a special deskunking bath.

Geriatric Care

There will come a time when you realize your Cocker Spaniel is a senior citizen. The dog may be 9 or 10 years old, perhaps younger or older. She may be having a little trouble getting up, or may be moving a little slower and sleeping more. The coat on some older dogs becomes quite gray, though this can start on very young dogs if they have a certain gene.

Many geriatric dogs become arthritic and need to be handled gently. After I developed arthritis I understood why some arthritic dogs are inclined to bite! Your veterinarian can prescribe medication to help relieve the pain.

Deafness is a problem that can result from chronic ear problems or advanced age. Deaf dogs respond well to hand signals, especially if they've learned them earlier in life. You need to be aware of a deaf dog's whereabouts at all times. If she wanders off, she's not going to respond to you calling her name. Also, be careful not to sneak up on a deaf dog; she can't hear you and could be startled.

The older dog's eyesight may diminish, or she may go completely blind. Blind dogs adjust amazingly well to their familiar environment. If your senior citizen is experiencing vision problems, she should be checked out by an ophthalmologist to make sure she is not in pain or that she doesn't need treatment.

Regular veterinary care is important for the geriatric dog. Your veterinarian may recommend a geriatric health profile starting at age 9 or 10. This profile might include a complete blood count, a blood chemistry profile, a urinalysis, a thyroid test, a chest X-ray, and an electrocardiogram. If any organ dysfunction is found, treatment can be started. This should be done every six months to a year for an old dog.

This is not the time to forego dental treatment! Anesthetics are safer than ever and, consequently, less stressful to the dog.

Some older dogs have periods of incontinence. Your veterinarian can prescribe medication that will help control this problem, but you need to give your older dog more opportunities to relieve herself.

It's best not to keep an older dog at a boarding kennel. You can make arrangements for her to be taken care of in her own home when you travel.

Some people may consider introducing a younger dog into the household. Years ago, I owned an ailing 10-year-old Cocker and purchased a puppy. That pup actually rejuvenated my old gal, and she lived another few years. However, you must be careful. Most senior citizens won't take too kindly to a rambunctious youngster. Whatever you do, make sure you pay more attention to your older dog than the newcomer.

Your old dog's senses may decline, causing behavior changes. Be extra tolerant of your senior Cocker Spaniel.

There may be a time when you have to make one of the hardest decisions in your life: when to end your dog's life. As much as we would prefer it, most aging dogs don't usually die quietly in their sleep. Eventually, we usually have to make a decision for them regarding euthanasia. Dogs seem to realize when they aren't the healthy animals they used to be. I don't think we should rob them of what little dignity they have left when their health goes. As loving pet owners, we need to spare our pets when possible. *Quality of life is what counts.* Remember the good times and say good-bye.

Part III

Enjoying Your Cocker Spaniel

Chapter 9

Training Your Cocker Spaniel

by Peggy Moran

Training makes your best friend better! A properly trained dog has a happier life and a longer life expectancy. He is also more appreciated by the people he encounters each day, both at home and out and about.

A trained dog walks nicely and joins his family often, going places untrained dogs cannot go. He is never rude or unruly, and he always happily comes when called. When he meets people for the first time, he greets them by sitting and waiting to be petted, rather than jumping up. At home he doesn't compete with his human family, and alone he is not destructive or overly anxious. He isn't continually nagged with words like "no," since he has learned not to misbehave in the first place. He is never shamed, harshly punished, or treated unkindly, and he is a well-loved, involved member of the family.

Sounds good, doesn't it? If you are willing to invest some time, thought, and patience, the words above could soon be used to describe your dog (though perhaps changing "he" to "she"). Educating your pet in a positive way is fun and easy, and there is no better gift you can give your pet than the guarantee of improved understanding and a great relationship.

This chapter will explain how to offer kind leadership, reshape your pet's behavior in a positive and practical way, and even get a head start on simple obedience training.

Understanding Builds the Bond

Dog training is a learning adventure on both ends of the leash. Before attempting to teach their dog new behaviors or change unwanted ones, thoughtful dog owners take the time to understand why their pets behave the way they do, and how their own behavior can be either a positive or negative influence on their dog.

Canine Nature

Loving dogs as much as we do, it's easy to forget they are a completely different species. Despite sharing our homes and living as appreciated members of our families, dogs do not think or learn exactly the same way people do. Even if you love your dog like a child, you must remember to respect the fact that he is actually a dog.

Dogs have no idea when their behavior is inappropriate from a human perspective. They are not aware of the value of possessions they chew or of messes they make or the worry they sometimes seem to cause. While people tend to look at behavior as good and bad or right and wrong, dogs just discover what works and what doesn't work. Then they behave accordingly, learning from their own experiences and increasing or reducing behaviors to improve results for themselves.

You might wonder, "But don't dogs want to please us"? My answer is yes, provided your pleasure reflects back to them in positive ways they can feel and appreciate. Dogs do things for *dog* reasons, and everything they do works for them in some way or they wouldn't be doing it!

The Social Dog

Our pets descended from animals who lived in tightly knit, cooperative social groups. Though far removed in appearance and lifestyle from their ancestors, our dogs still relate in many of the same ways their wild relatives did. And in their relationships with one another, wild canids either lead or follow.

Canine ranking relationships are not about cruelty and power; they are about achievement and abilities. Competent dogs with high levels of drive and confidence step up, while deferring dogs step aside. But followers don't get the short end of the stick; they benefit from the security of having a more competent dog at the helm.

Our domestic dogs still measure themselves against other members of their group—us! Dog owners whose actions lead to positive results have willing, secure followers. But dogs may step up and fill the void or cut loose and do their own thing when their people fail to show capable leadership. When dogs are pushy, aggressive, and rude, or independent and unwilling, it's not because they have designs on the role of "master." It is more likely their owners failed to provide consistent leadership.

Dogs in training benefit from their handler's good leadership. Their education flows smoothly because they are impressed. Being in charge doesn't require you to physically dominate or punish your dog. You simply need to make some subtle changes in the way you relate to him every day.

Lead Your Pack!

Create schedules and structure daily activities. Dogs are creatures of habit and routines will create security. Feed meals at the same times each day and also try to schedule regular walks, training practices, and toilet outings. Your predictability will help your dog be patient.

Ask your dog to perform a task. Before releasing him to food or freedom, have him do something as simple as sit on command. Teach him that cooperation earns great results!

Give a release prompt (such as "let's go") when going through doors leading outside. This is a better idea than allowing your impatient pup to rush past you.

Pet your dog when he is calm, not when he is excited. Turn your touch into a tool that relaxes and settles.

Reward desirable rather than inappropriate behavior. Petting a jumping dog (who hasn't been invited up) reinforces jumping. Pet sitting dogs, and only invite lap dogs up after they've first "asked" by waiting for your invitation.

Replace personal punishment with positive reinforcement. Show a dog what *to do,* and motivate him to want to do it, and there will be no need to punish him for what he should *not do.* Dogs naturally follow, without the need for force or harshness.

Play creatively and appropriately. Your dog will learn the most about his social rank when he is playing with you. During play, dogs work to control toys and try to get the best of one another in a friendly way. The wrong sorts of play can create problems: For example, tug of war can lead to aggressiveness. Allowing your dog to control toys during play may result in possessive guarding when he has something he really values, such as a bone. Dogs who are chased during play may later run away from you when you approach to leash them. The right kinds of play will help increase your dog's social confidence while you gently assert your leadership.

How Dogs Learn (and How They Don't)

Dog training begins as a meeting of minds—yours and your dog's. Though the end goal may be to get your dog's body to behave in a specific way, training starts as a mind game. Your dog is learning all the time by observing the consequences of his actions and social interactions. He is always seeking out what he perceives as desirable and trying to avoid what he perceives as undesirable.

He will naturally repeat a behavior that either brings him more good stuff or makes bad stuff go away (these are both types of reinforcement). He will naturally avoid a behavior that brings him more bad stuff or makes the good stuff go away (these are both types of punishment).

Both reinforcement and punishment can be perceived as either the direct result of something the dog did himself, or as coming from an outside source.

Using Life's Rewards

Your best friend is smart and he is also cooperative. When the best things in life can only be had by working with you, your dog will view you as a facilitator. You unlock doors to all of the positively reinforcing experiences he values: his freedom, his friends at the park, food, affection, walks, and play. The trained dog accompanies you through those doors and waits to see what working with you will bring.

Rewarding your dog for good behavior is called positive reinforcement, and, as we've just seen, it increases the likelihood that he will repeat that behavior. The perfect reward is anything your dog wants that is safe and appropriate. Don't limit yourself to toys, treats, and things that come directly from you. Harness life's positives—barking at squirrels, chasing a falling leaf, bounding away from you at the dog park, pausing for a moment to sniff everything—and allow your dog to earn access to those things as rewards that come from cooperating with you. When he looks at you, when he sits, when he comes when you call—any prompted behavior can earn one of life's rewards. When he works with you, he earns the things he most appreciates; but when he tries to get those things on his own, he cannot. Rather than seeing you as someone who always says "no," your dog will view you as the one who says "let's go!" He will *want* to follow.

What About Punishment?

Not only is it unnecessary to personally punish dogs, it is abusive. No matter how convinced you are that your dog "knows right from wrong," in reality he will associate personal punishment with the punisher. The resulting cowering, "guilty"-looking postures are actually displays of submission and fear. Later,

Purely Positive Reinforcement

With positive training, we emphasize teaching dogs what they should do to earn reinforcements, rather than punishing them for unwanted behaviors.

- Focus on teaching "do" rather than "don't." For example, a sitting dog isn't jumping.
- Use positive reinforcers that are valuable to your dog and the situation: A tired dog values rest; a confined dog values freedom.
- Play (appropriately)!
- Be a consistent leader.
- Set your dog up for success by anticipating and preventing problems.
- Notice and reward desirable behavior, and give him lots of attention when he is being good.
- Train ethically. Use humane methods and equipment that do not frighten or hurt your dog.
- When you are angry, walk away and plan a positive strategy.
- Keep practice sessions short and sweet. Five to ten minutes, three to five times a day is best.

when the punisher isn't around and the coast is clear, the same behavior he was punished for—such as raiding a trash can—might bring a self-delivered, very tasty result. The punished dog hasn't learned not to misbehave; he has learned to not get caught.

Does punishment ever have a place in dog training? Many people will heartily insist it does not. But dog owners often get frustrated as they try to stick to the path of all-positive reinforcement. It sure sounds great, but is it realistic, or even natural, to *never* say "no" to your dog?

A wild dog's life is not *all* positive. Hunger and thirst are both examples of negative reinforcement; the resulting discomfort motivates the wild dog to seek food and water. He encounters natural aversives such as pesky insects; mats in his coat; cold days; rainy days; sweltering hot days; and occasional run-ins with thorns, brambles, skunks, bees, and other nastiness. These all affect his behavior, as he tries to avoid the bad stuff whenever possible. The wild dog also occasionally encounters social punishers from others in his group when he gets too pushy. Starting with a growl or a snap from Mom, and later some mild and ritualized discipline from other members of his four-legged family, he learns to modify behaviors that elicit grouchy responses.

Our pet dogs don't naturally experience all positive results either, because they learn from their surroundings and from social experiences with other dogs. Watch a group of pet dogs playing together and you'll see a very old educational system still being used. As they wrestle and attempt to assert themselves, you'll notice many mouth-on-neck moments. Their playful biting is inhibited, with no intention to cause harm, but their message is clear: "Say uncle or this could hurt more!"

Observing that punishment does occur in nature, some people may feel compelled to try to be like the big wolf with their pet dogs. Becoming aggressive or heavy-handed with your pet will backfire! Your dog will not be impressed, nor will he want to follow you. Punishment causes dogs to change their behavior to avoid or escape discomfort and threats. Threatened dogs will either become very passive and offer submissive, appeasing postures, attempt to flee, or rise to the occasion and fight back. When people personally punish their dogs in an angry manner, one of these three defensive mechanisms will be triggered. Which one depends on a dog's genetic temperament as well as his past social experiences. Since we don't want to make our pets feel the need to avoid or escape us, personal punishment has no place in our training.

Remote Consequences

Sometimes, however, all-positive reinforcement is just not enough. That's because not all reinforcement comes from us. An inappropriate behavior can be self-reinforcing—just doing it makes the dog feel better in some way, whether you are there to say "good boy!" or not. Some examples are eating garbage, pulling the stuffing out of your sofa, barking at passersby, or urinating on the floor.

Although you don't want to personally punish your dog, the occasional deterrent may be called for to help derail these kinds of self-rewarding misbehaviors. In these cases, mild forms of impersonal or remote punishment can be used as part of a correction. The goal isn't to make your dog feel bad or to "know he has done wrong," but to help redirect him to alternate behaviors that are more acceptable to you.

The Problems with Personal Punishment

- Personally punished dogs are not taught appropriate behaviors.
- Personally punished dogs only stop misbehaving when they are caught or interrupted, but they don't learn not to misbehave when they are alone.
- Personally punished dogs become shy, fearful, and distrusting.
- Personally punished dogs may become defensively aggressive.
- Personally punished dogs become suppressed and inhibited.
- Personally punished dogs become stressed, triggering stress-reducing behaviors that their owners interpret as acts of spite, triggering even more punishment.
- Personally punished dogs have stressed owners.
- Personally punished dogs may begin to repeat behaviors they have been taught will result in negative, but predictable, attention.
- Personally punished dogs are more likely to be given away than are positively trained dogs.

You do this by pairing a slightly startling, totally impersonal sound with an equally impersonal and *very mild* remote consequence. The impersonal sound might be a single shake of an empty plastic pop bottle with pennies in it, held out of your dog's sight. Or you could use a vocal expression such as "eh!" delivered with you looking *away* from your misbehaving dog.

Pair your chosen sound—the penny bottle or "eh!"—with either a slight tug on his collar or a sneaky spritz on the rump from a water bottle. Do this right *as* he touches something he should not; bad timing will confuse your dog and undermine your training success.

To keep things under your control and make sure you get the timing right, it's best to do this as a setup. "Accidentally" drop a shoe on the floor, and then help your dog learn some things are best avoided. As he sniffs the shoe say "eh!" without looking at him and give a *slight* tug against his collar. This sound will quickly become meaningful as a correction all by itself—sometimes after just one setup—making the tug correction obsolete. The tug lets your dog see that you were right; going for that shoe *was* a bad idea! Your wise dog will be more likely to heed your warning next time, and probably move closer to you where it's safe. Be a good friend and pick up the nasty shoe. He'll be relieved and you'll look heroic. Later, when he's home alone and encounters a stray shoe, he'll want to give it a wide berth.

Your negative marking sound will come in handy in the future, when your dog begins to venture down the wrong behavioral path. The goal is not to announce your disapproval or to threaten your dog. You are not telling him to stop or showing how *you* feel about his behavior. You are sounding a warning to a friend who's venturing off toward danger—"I wouldn't if I were you!" Suddenly, there is an abrupt, rather startling, noise! Now is the moment to redirect him and help him earn positive reinforcement. That interrupted behavior will become something he wants to avoid in the future, but he won't want to avoid you.

Practical Commands for Family Pets

Before you begin training your dog, let's look at some equipment you'll want to have on hand:

- **A buckle collar** is fine for most dogs. If your dog pulls *very* hard, try a head collar, a device similar to a horse halter that helps reduce pulling by turning the dog's head. *Do not* use a choke chain (sometimes called a training collar), because they cause physical harm even when used correctly.
- **Six-foot training leash and twenty-six–foot retractable leash.**
- **A few empty plastic soda bottles with about twenty pennies in each one.** This will be used to impersonally interrupt misbehaviors before redirecting dogs to more positive activities.
- **A favorite squeaky toy,** to motivate, attract attention, and reward your dog during training.

Lure your dog to take just a few steps with you on the leash by being inviting and enthusiastic. Make sure you reward him for his efforts.

Baby Steps

Allow your young pup to drag a short, lightweight leash attached to a buckle collar for a few *supervised* moments, several times each day. At first the leash may annoy him and he may jump around a bit trying to get away from it. Distract him with your squeaky toy or a bit of his kibble and he'll quickly get used to his new "tail."

Begin walking him on the leash by holding the end and following him. As he adapts, you can begin to assert gentle direct pressure to teach him to follow you. Don't jerk or yank, or he will become afraid to walk when the leash is on. If he becomes hesitant, squat down facing him and let him figure out that by moving toward you he is safe and secure. If he remains confused or frightened and doesn't come to you, go to him and help him understand that you provide safe harbor while he's on the leash. Then back away a few steps and try again to lure him to you. As he learns that you are the "home base," he'll want to follow when you walk a few steps, waiting for you to stop, squat down, and make him feel great.

So Attached to You!

The next step in training your dog—and this is a very important one—is to begin spending at least an hour or more each day with him on a four- to six-foot leash, held by or tethered to you. This training will increase his attachment to you—literally!—as you sit quietly or walk about, tending to your household business. When you are quiet, he'll learn it is time to settle; when you are active, he'll learn to move with you. Tethering also keeps him out of trouble when you are busy but still want his company. It is a great alternative to confining a dog, and can be used instead of crating any time you're home and need to slow him down a bit.

Rotating your dog from supervised freedom to tethered time to some quiet time in the crate or his gated area gives him a diverse and balanced day while he is learning. Two confined or tethered hours is the most you should require of your dog in one stretch, before changing to some supervised freedom, play, or a walk.

The dog in training may, at times, be stressed by all of the changes he is dealing with. Provide a stress outlet, such as a toy to chew on, when he is confined or tethered. He will settle into his quiet time more quickly and completely. Always be sure to provide several rounds of daily play and free time (in a fenced area or on your retractable leash) in addition to plenty of chewing materials.

Dog Talk

Dogs don't speak in words, but they do have a language—body language. They use postures, vocalizations, movements, facial gestures,

Tethering your dog is great way to keep him calm and under control, but still with you.

odors, and touch—usually with their mouths—to communicate what they are feeling and thinking.

We also "speak" using body language. We have quite an array of postures, movements, and facial gestures that accompany our touch and language as we attempt to communicate with our pets. And our dogs can quickly figure us out!

Alone, without associations, words are just noises. But, because we pair them with meaningful body language, our dogs make the connection. Dogs can really learn to understand much of what we *say,* if what we *do* at the same time is consistent.

The Positive Marker

Start your dog's education with one of the best tricks in dog training: Pair various positive reinforcers—food, a toy, touch—with a sound such as a click on a clicker (which you can get at the pet supply store) or a spoken word like "good!" or "yes!" This will enable you to later "mark" your dog's desirable behaviors.

It seems too easy: Just say "yes!" and give the dog his toy. (Or use whatever sound and reward you have chosen.) Later, when you make your marking sound right at the instant your dog does the right thing, he will know you are going to be giving him something good for that particular action. And he'll be eager to repeat the behavior to hear you mark it again!

Next, you must teach your dog to understand the meaning of cues you'll be using to ask him to perform specific behaviors. This is easy, too. Does he already do things you might like him to do on command? Of course! He lies down, he sits, he picks things up, he drops them again, he comes to you. All of the behaviors you'd like to control are already part of your dog's natural repertoire. The trick is getting him to offer those behaviors when you ask for them. And that means you have to teach him to associate a particular behavior on his part with a particular behavior on your part.

Sit Happens

Teach your dog an important new rule: From now on, he is only touched and petted when he is either sitting or lying down. You won't need to ask him to sit; in fact, you should not. Just keeping him tethered near you so there isn't much to do but stand, be ignored, or settle, and wait until sit happens.

He may pester you a bit, but be stoic and unresponsive. Starting now, when *you* are sitting down, a sitting dog is the only one you see and pay attention to. He will eventually sit, and as he does, attach the word "sit"—but don't be too excited or he'll jump right back up. Now mark with your positive sound that promises something good, then reward him with a slow, quiet, settling pet.

Training requires consistent reinforcement. Ask others to also wait until your dog is sitting and calm to touch him, and he will associate being petted with being relaxed. Be sure you train your dog to associate everyone's touch with quiet bonding.

Reinforcing "Sit" as a Command

Since your dog now understands one concept of working for a living—sit to earn petting—you can begin to shape and reinforce his desire to sit. Hold toys, treats, his bowl of food, and turn into a statue. But don't prompt him to sit! Instead, remain frozen and unavailable, looking somewhere out into space, over his head. He will put on a bit of a show, trying to get a response from you, and may offer various behaviors, but only one will push your button—sitting. Wait for him to offer the "right" behavior, and when he does, you unfreeze. Say "sit," then mark with an excited "good!" and give him the toy or treat with a release command—"OK!"

When you notice spontaneous sits occurring, be sure to take advantage of those free opportunities to make your command sequence meaningful and positive. Say "sit" as you observe sit happen—then mark with "good!" and praise, pet, or reward the dog. Soon, every time you look at your dog he'll be sitting and looking right back at you!

Now, after thirty days of purely positive practice, it's time to give him a test. When he is just walking around doing his own thing, suddenly ask him to sit. He'll probably do it right away. If he doesn't, do *not* repeat your command, or you'll just undermine its meaning ("sit" means sit *now;* the command is not "sit, sit, sit, sit"). Instead, get something he likes and let him know you have it. Wait for him to offer the sit—he will—then say "sit!" and complete your marking and rewarding sequence.

OK

"OK" will probably rate as one of your dog's favorite words. It's like the word "recess" to schoolchildren. It is the word used to release your dog from a command. You can introduce "OK" during your "sit" practice. When he gets up from a sit, say "OK" to tell him the sitting is finished. Soon that sound will mean "freedom."

Make it even more meaningful and positive. Whenever he spontaneously bounds away, say "OK!" Squeak a toy, and when he notices and shows interest, toss it for him.

Down

I've mentioned that you should only pet your dog when he is either sitting or lying down. Now, using the approach I've just introduced for "sit," teach your dog to lie down. You will be a statue, and hold something he would like to get but that you'll only release to a dog who is lying down. It helps to lower the desired item to the floor in front of him, still not speaking and not letting him have it until he offers you the new behavior you are seeking.

Lower your dog's reward to the floor to help him figure out what behavior will earn him his reward.

He may offer a sit and then wait expectantly, but you must make him keep searching for the new trick that triggers your generosity. Allow your dog to experiment and find the right answer, even if he has to search around for it first. When he lands on "down" and learns it is another behavior that works, he'll offer it more quickly the next time.

Don't say "down" until he lies down, to tightly associate your prompt with the correct behavior. To say "down, down, down" as he is sitting, looking at you, or pawing at the toy would make "down" mean those behaviors instead! Whichever behavior he offers, a training opportunity has been created. Once you've attached and shaped both sitting and lying down, you can ask for both behaviors with your verbal prompts, "sit" or "down." Be sure to only reinforce the "correct" reply!

Stay

"Stay" can easily be taught as an extension of what you've already been practicing. To teach "stay," you follow the entire sequence for reinforcing a "sit" or "down," except you wait a bit longer before you give the release word, "OK!" Wait a second or two longer during each practice before saying "OK!" and releasing your dog to the positive reinforcer (toy, treat, or one of life's other rewards).

You can step on the leash to help your dog understand the down-stay, but only do this when he is already lying down. You don't want to hurt him!

If he gets up before you've said "OK," you have two choices: pretend the release was your idea and quickly interject "OK!" as he breaks; or, if he is more experienced and practiced, mark the behavior with your correction sound—"eh!"— and then gently put him back on the spot, wait for him to lie down, and begin again. Be sure the next three practices are a success. Ask him to wait for just a second, and release him before he can be wrong. You need to keep your dog feeling like more of a success than a failure as you begin to test his training in increasingly more distracting and difficult situations.

As he gets the hang of it—he stays until you say "OK"— you can gradually push for longer times—up to a minute on a sit-stay, and up to three minutes on a down-stay. You can also gradually add distractions and work in new environments. To add a minor self-correction for the down-stay, stand on the dog's leash after he lies down, allowing about three inches of slack. If he tries to get up before you've said "OK," he'll discover it doesn't work.

Do not step on the leash to make your dog lie down! This could badly hurt his neck, and will destroy his trust in you. Remember, we are teaching our dogs to make the best choices, not inflicting our answers upon them!

Come

Rather than thinking of "come" as an action—"come to me"—think of it as a place—"the dog is sitting in front of me, facing me." Since your dog by now really likes sitting to earn your touch and other positive reinforcement, he's likely to sometimes sit directly in front of you, facing you, all on his own. When this happens, give it a specific name: "come."

Now follow the rest of the training steps you have learned to make him like doing it and reinforce the behavior by practicing it any chance you get. Anything your dog wants and likes could be earned as a result of his first offering the sit-in-front known as "come."

You can help guide him into the right location. Use your hands as "landing gear" and pat the insides of your legs at his nose level. Do this while backing up a bit, to help him maneuver to the straight-in-front, facing-you position. Don't say the

Pat the insides of your legs to show your dog exactly where you like him to sit when you say "come."

word "come" while he's maneuvering, because he hasn't! You are trying to make "come" the end result, not the work in progress.

You can also help your dog by marking his movement in the right direction: Use your positive sound or word to promise he is getting warm. When he finally sits facing you, enthusiastically say "come," mark again with your positive word, and release him with an enthusiastic "OK!" Make it so worth his while, with lots of play and praise, that he can't wait for you to ask him to come again!

Building a Better Recall

Practice, practice, practice. Now, practice some more. Teach your dog that all good things in life hinge upon him first sitting in front of you in a behavior named "come." When you think he really has got it, test him by asking him to "come" as you gradually add distractions and change locations. Expect setbacks as you make these changes and practice accordingly. Lower your expectations and make his task easier so he is able to get it right. Use those distractions as rewards, when they are appropriate. For example, let him check out the interesting leaf that blew by as a reward for first coming to you and ignoring it.

Add distance and call your dog to come while he is on his retractable leash. If he refuses and sits looking at you blankly, *do not* jerk, tug, "pop," or reel him in. Do nothing! It is his move; wait to see what behavior he offers. He'll either begin to approach (mark the behavior with an excited "good!"), sit and do nothing (just keep waiting), or he'll try to move in some direction other than toward you. If he tries to leave, use your correction marker—"eh!"— and bring him to a stop by letting him walk to the end of the leash, *not* by jerking him. Now walk to him in a neutral manner, and don't jerk or show any disapproval. Gently bring him back to the spot where he was when you called him, then back away and face him, still waiting and not reissuing your command. Let him keep examining his options until he finds the one that works—yours!

If you have practiced everything I've suggested so far and given your dog a chance to really learn what "come" means, he is well aware of what you want and is quite intelligently weighing all his options. The only way he'll know your way is the one that works is to be allowed to examine his other choices and discover that they *don't* work.

Sooner or later every dog tests his training. Don't be offended or angry when your dog tests you. No matter how positive you've made it, he won't always want to do everything you ask, every time. When he explores the "what happens if I don't" scenario, your training is being strengthened. He will discover through his own process of trial and error that the best—and only—way out of a command he really doesn't feel compelled to obey is to obey it.

Let's Go

Many pet owners wonder if they can retain control while walking their dogs and still allow at least some running in front, sniffing, and playing. You might worry that allowing your dog occasional freedom could result in him expecting it all the time, leading to a testy, leash-straining walk. It's possible for both parties on the leash to have an enjoyable experience by implementing and reinforcing well-thought-out training techniques.

Begin by making word associations you'll use on your walks. Give the dog some slack on the leash, and as he starts to walk away from you say "OK" and begin to follow him.

Do not let him drag you; set the pace even when he is being given a turn at being the leader. Whenever he starts to pull, just come to a standstill and refuse to move (or refuse to allow him to continue forward) until there is slack in the leash. Do this correction without saying anything at all. When he isn't pulling, you may decide to just stand still and let him sniff about within the range the slack leash allows, or you may even mosey along following him. After a few minutes of "recess," it is time to work. Say something like "that's it" or "time's up," close the distance between you and your dog, and touch him.

Next say "let's go" (or whatever command you want to use to mean "follow me as we walk"). Turn and walk off, and, if he follows, mark his behavior with "good!" Then stop,

Give your dog slack on his leash as you walk and let him make the decision to walk with you.

When your dog catches up with you, make sure you let him know what a great dog he is!

Intersperse periods of attentive walking, where your dog is on a shorter leash, with periods on a slack leash, where he is allowed to look and sniff around.

squat down, and let him catch you. Make him glad he did! Start again, and do a few transitions as he gets the hang of your follow-the-leader game, speeding up, slowing down, and trying to make it fun. When you stop, he gets to catch up and receive some deserved positive reinforcement. Don't forget that's the reason he is following you, so be sure to make it worth his while!

Require him to remain attentive to you. Do not allow sniffing, playing, eliminating, or pulling during your time as leader on a walk. If he seems to get distracted—which, by the way, is the main reason dogs walk poorly with their people—change direction or pace without saying a word. Just help him realize "oops, I lost track of my human." Do not jerk his neck and say "heel"—this will make the word "heel" mean pain in the neck and will not encourage him to cooperate with you. Don't repeat "let's go," either. He needs to figure out that it is his job to keep track of and follow you if he wants to earn the positive benefits you provide.

The best reward you can give a dog for performing an attentive, controlled walk is a few minutes of walking without all of the controls. Of course, he must remain on a leash even during the "recess" parts of the walk, but allowing him to discriminate between attentive following—"let's go"—and having a few moments of relaxation—"OK"—will increase his willingness to work.

Training for Attention

Your dog pretty much has a one-track mind. Once he is focused on something, everything else is excluded. This can be great, for instance, when he's focusing on you! But it can also be dangerous if, for example, his attention is riveted on the bunny he is chasing and he does not hear you call—that is, not unless he has been trained to pay attention when you say his name.

When you say your dog's name, you'll want him to make eye contact with you. Begin teaching this by making yourself so intriguing that he can't help but look.

When you call your dog's name, you will again be seeking a specific response—eye contact. The best way to teach this is to trigger his alerting response by making a noise with your mouth, such as whistling or a kissing sound, and then immediately doing something he'll find very intriguing.

You can play a treasure hunt game to help teach him to regard his name as a request for attention. As a bonus, you can reinforce the rest of his new vocabulary at the same time.

Treasure Hunt

Make a kissing sound, then jump up and find a dog toy or dramatically raid the fridge and rather noisily eat a piece of cheese. After doing this twice, make a kissing sound and then look at your dog.

Of course he is looking at you! He is waiting to see if that sound—the kissing sound—means you're going to go hunting again. After all, you're so good at it! Because he is looking, say his name, mark with "good," then go hunting and find his toy. Release it to him with an "OK." At any point if he follows you, attach your "let's go!" command; if he leaves you, give permission with "OK."

Using this approach, he cannot be wrong—any behavior your dog offers can be named. You can add things like "take it" when he picks up a toy, and "thank you" when he happens to drop one. Many opportunities to make your new vocabulary meaningful and positive can be found within this simple training game.

Problems to watch out for when teaching the treasure hunt:

- You really do not want your dog to come to you when you call his name (later, when you try to engage his attention to ask him to stay, he'll already be on his way toward you). You just want him to look at you.
- Saying "watch me, watch me" doesn't teach your dog to *offer* his attention. It just makes you a background noise.
- Don't lure your dog's attention with the reward. Get his attention and then reward him for looking. Try holding a toy in one hand with your arm stretched out to your side. Wait until he looks at you rather than the toy. Now say his name then mark with "good!" and release the toy. As he goes for it, say "OK."

To get your dog's attention, try holding his toy with your arm out to your side. Wait until he looks at you, then mark the moment and give him the toy.

Teaching Cooperation

Never punish your dog for failing to obey you or try to punish him into compliance. Bribing, repeating yourself, and doing a behavior for him all avoid the real issue of dog training—his will. He must be helped to be willing, not made to achieve tasks. Good dog training helps your dog want to obey. He learns that he can gain what he values most through cooperation and compliance, and can't gain those things any other way.

Your dog is learning to *earn,* rather than expect, the good things in life. And you've become much more important to him than you were before. Because you are allowing him to experiment and learn, he doesn't have to be forced, manipulated, or bribed. When he wants something, he can gain it by cooperating with you. One of those "somethings"—and a great reward you shouldn't underestimate—is your positive attention, paid to him with love and sincere approval!

Chapter 10

Housetraining Your Cocker Spaniel

Excerpted from Housetraining: An Owner's Guide to a Happy Healthy Pet, 1st Edition, *by September Morn*

By the time puppies are about 3 weeks old, they start to follow their mother around. When they are a few steps away from their clean sleeping area, the mama dog stops. The pups try to nurse but mom won't allow it. The pups mill around in frustration, then nature calls and they all urinate and defecate here, away from their bed. The mother dog returns to the nest, with her brood waddling behind her. Their first housetraining lesson has been a success.

The next one to housetrain puppies should be their breeder. The breeder watches as the puppies eliminate, then deftly removes the soiled papers and replaces them with clean papers before the pups can traipse back through their messes. He has wisely arranged the puppies' space so their bed, food, and drinking water are as far away from the elimination area as possible. This way, when the pups follow their mama, they will move away from their sleeping and eating area before eliminating. This habit will help the pups be easily housetrained.

Your Housetraining Shopping List

While your puppy's mother and breeder are getting her started on good housetraining habits, you'll need to do some shopping. If you have all the essentials in place before your dog arrives, it will be easier to help her learn the rules from day one.

Newspaper: The younger your puppy and larger her breed, the more newspapers you'll need. Newspaper is absorbent, abundant, cheap, and convenient.

Puddle Pads: If you prefer not to stockpile newspaper, a commercial alternative is puddle pads. These thick paper pads can be purchased under several trade names at pet supply stores. The pads have waterproof backing, so puppy urine doesn't seep through onto the floor. Their disadvantages are that they will cost you more than newspapers and that they contain plastics that are not biodegradable.

Poop Removal Tool: There are several types of poop removal tools available. Some are designed with a separate pan and rake, and others have the handles hinged like scissors. Some scoops need two hands for operation, while others are designed for one-handed use. Try out the different brands at your pet supply store. Put a handful of pebbles or dog kibble on the floor and then pick them up with each type of scoop to determine which works best for you.

Plastic Bags: When you take your dog outside your yard, you *must* pick up after her. Dog waste is unsightly, smelly, and can harbor disease. In many cities and towns, the law mandates dog owners clean up pet waste deposited on public ground. Picking up after your dog using a plastic bag scoop is simple. Just put your hand inside the bag, like a mitten, and then grab the droppings. Turn the bag inside out, tie the top, and that's that.

Crate: To housetrain a puppy, you will need some way to confine her when you're unable to supervise. A dog crate is a secure way to confine your dog for short periods during the day and to use as a comfortable bed at night. Crates come in wire mesh and in plastic. The wire ones are foldable to store flat in a smaller space. The plastic ones are more cozy, draft-free, and quiet, and are approved for airline travel.

Baby Gates: Since you shouldn't crate a dog for more than an hour or two at a time during the day, baby gates are a good way to limit your dog's freedom in the house. Be sure the baby gates you use are safe. The old-fashioned wooden, expanding lattice type has seriously injured a number of children by collapsing and trapping a leg, arm, or neck. That type of gate can hurt a puppy, too, so use the modern grid type gates instead. You'll need more than one baby gate if you have several doorways to close off.

Exercise Pen: Portable exercise pens are great when you have a young pup or a small dog. These metal or plastic pens are made of rectangular panels that are hinged together. The pens are freestanding, sturdy, foldable, and can be carried like a suitcase. You could set one up in your kitchen as the pup's daytime corral, and then take it outdoors to contain your pup while you garden or just sit and enjoy the day.

Enzymatic Cleaner: All dogs make housetraining mistakes. Accept this and be ready for it by buying an enzymatic cleaner made especially for pet accidents. Dogs like to eliminate where they have done it before, and lingering smells lead them to those spots. Ordinary household cleaners may remove all the odors you can smell, but only an enzymatic cleaner will remove everything your dog can smell.

The First Day

Housetraining is a matter of establishing good habits in your dog. That means you never want her to learn anything she will eventually have to unlearn. Start off housetraining on the right foot by teaching your dog that you prefer her to eliminate outside. Designate a potty area in your backyard (if you have one) or in the street in front of your home and take your dog to it as soon as you arrive home. Let her sniff a bit and, when she squats to go, give the action a name: "potty" or "do it" or anything else you won't be embarrassed to say in public. Eventually your dog will associate that word with the act and will eliminate on command. When she's finished, praise her with "good potty!"

Take your pup out frequently to her special potty spot and praise her when she goes.

That first day, take your puppy out to the potty area frequently. Although she may not eliminate every time, you are establishing a routine: You take her to her spot, ask her to eliminate, and praise her when she does.

Just before bedtime, take your dog to her potty area once more. Stand by and wait until she produces. Do not put your

Don't Overuse the Crate

A crate serves well as a dog's overnight bed, but you should not leave the dog in her crate for more than an hour or two during the day. Throughout the day, she needs to play and exercise. She is likely to want to drink some water and will undoubtedly eliminate. Confining your dog all day will give her no option but to soil her crate. This is not just unpleasant for you and the dog, but it reinforces bad cleanliness habits. And crating a pup for the whole day is abusive. Don't do it.

dog to bed for the night until she has eliminated. Be patient and calm. This is not the time to play with or excite your dog. If she's too excited, a pup not only won't eliminate, she probably won't want to sleep either.

Most dogs, even young ones, will not soil their beds if they can avoid it. For this reason, a sleeping crate can be a tremendous help during housetraining. Being crated at night can help a dog develop the muscles that control elimination. So after your dog has emptied out, put her to bed in her crate.

A good place to put your dog's sleeping crate is near your own bed. Dogs are pack animals, so they feel safer sleeping with others in a common area. In your bedroom, the pup will be near you and you'll be close enough to hear when she wakes during the night and needs to eliminate.

Pups under 4 months old often are not able to hold their urine all night. If your puppy has settled down to sleep but awakens and fusses a few hours later, she probably needs to go out. For the best housetraining progress, take your pup to her elimination area whenever she needs to go, even in the wee hours of the morning.

Your dog's crate is a great housetraining tool.

Your pup may soil in her crate if you ignore her late night urgency. It's unfair to let this happen, and it sends the wrong message about your expectations for cleanliness. Resign yourself to this midnight outing and just get up and take the pup out. Your pup will outgrow this need soon and will learn in the process that she can count on you, and you'll wake happily each morning to a clean dog.

The next morning, the very first order of business is to take your pup out to eliminate. Don't forget to take her to her special potty spot, ask her to eliminate, and then praise her when she does. After your pup empties out in the morning, give her breakfast, and then take her to her potty area again. After that, she shouldn't need to eliminate again right away, so you can allow her some free playtime. Keep an eye on the pup though, because when she pauses in play she may need to go potty. Take her to the right spot, give the command, and praise if she produces.

Confine Your Pup

A pup or dog who has not finished housetraining should *never* be allowed the run of the house unattended. A new dog (especially a puppy) with unlimited access to your house will make her own choices about where to eliminate. Vigilance during your new dog's first few weeks in your home will pay big dividends. Every potty mistake delays housetraining progress; every success speeds it along.

> **TIP**
>
> **Water**
>
> Make sure your dog has access to clean water at all times. Limiting the amount of water a dog drinks is not necessary for housetraining success and can be very dangerous. A dog needs water to digest food, to maintain a proper body temperature and proper blood volume, and to clean her system of toxins and wastes. A healthy dog will automatically drink the right amount. Do not restrict water intake. Controlling your dog's access to water is not the key to housetraining her; controlling her access to everything else in your home is.

Prevent problems by setting up a controlled environment for your new pet. A good place for a puppy corral is often the kitchen. Kitchens almost always have waterproof or easily cleaned floors, which is a distinct asset with leaky pups. A bathroom, laundry room, or enclosed porch could be used for a puppy corral, but the kitchen is generally the best location. Kitchens are a meeting place and a hub of activity for many families, and a puppy will learn better manners when she is socialized thoroughly with family, friends, and nice strangers.

The way you structure your pup's corral area is very important. Her bed, food, and water should be at the opposite end of the corral from the potty area. When you first get your pup, spread newspaper over the rest of the floor of her playpen corral. Lay the papers at least four pages thick and be sure to overlap the edges. As you note the pup's progress, you can remove the papers nearest the sleeping and eating corner. Gradually decrease the size of the papered area until only the end where you want the pup to eliminate is covered. If you will be training your dog to eliminate outside, place newspaper at the end of the corral that is closest to the door that leads outdoors. That way as she moves away from the clean area to the papered area, the pup will also form the habit of heading toward the door to go out.

This pup is in a big pen with a plastic covering on the floor. Don't give your puppy freedom to get into trouble.

Maintain a scent marker for the pup's potty area by reserving a small soiled piece of paper when you clean up. Place this piece, with her scent of urine, under the top sheet of the clean papers you spread. This will cue your pup where to eliminate.

Most dog owners use a combination of indoor papers and outdoor elimination areas. When the pup is left by herself in the corral, she can potty on the ever-present newspaper. When you are available to take the pup outside, she can do her business in the outdoor spot. It is not difficult to switch a pup from indoor paper training to outdoor elimination. Owners of large pups often switch early, but potty papers are still useful if the pup spends time in her indoor corral while you're away. Use the papers as long as your pup needs them. If you come home and they haven't been soiled, you are ahead.

When setting up your pup's outdoor yard, put the lounging area as far away as possible from the potty area, just as with the indoor corral setup. People with large yards, for example, might leave a patch unmowed at the edge of the lawn to serve as the dog's elimination area. Other dog owners teach the dog to relieve herself in a designated corner of a deck or patio. For an apartment-dwelling city dog, the outdoor potty area might be a tiny balcony or the curb. Each dog owner has somewhat different expectations for their dog. Teach your dog to eliminate in a spot that suits your environment and lifestyle.

Take your dog outside frequently to eliminate. Stay with her and make sure she goes. Praise her when she does.

Be sure to pick up droppings in your yard at least once a day. Dogs have a natural desire to stay far away from their own excrement, and if too many piles litter the ground, your dog won't want to walk through it and will start eliminating elsewhere. Leave just one small piece of feces in the potty area to remind your dog where the right spot is located.

To help a pup adapt to the change from indoors to outdoors, take one of her potty papers outside to the new elimination area. Let the pup stand on the paper when she goes potty outdoors. Each day for four days, reduce the size of the paper by half. By the fifth day, the pup, having used a smaller and smaller piece of paper to stand on, will probably just go to that spot and eliminate.

Take your pup to her outdoor potty place frequently throughout the day. A puppy can hold her urine for only about as many hours as her age in months, and will move her bowels as many times a day as she eats. So a 2-month-old pup will urinate about every two hours, while at 4 months she can manage about four hours between piddles. Pups vary somewhat in their rate of development, so this is not a hard and fast rule. It does, however, present a realistic idea of how long a pup can be left without access to a potty place. Past 4 months, her potty trips will be less frequent.

When you take the dog outdoors to her spot, keep her leashed so that she won't wander away. Stand quietly and let her sniff around in the designated area.

If your pup starts to leave before she has eliminated, gently lead her back and remind her to go. If your pup sniffs at the spot, praise her calmly, say the command word, and just wait. If she produces, praise serenely, then give her time to sniff around a little more. She may not be finished, so give her time to go again before allowing her to play and explore her new home.

If you find yourself waiting more than five minutes for your dog to potty, take her back inside. Watch your pup carefully for twenty minutes, not giving her any opportunity to slip away to eliminate unnoticed. If you are too busy to watch the pup, put her in her crate. After twenty minutes, take her to the outdoor potty spot again and tell her what to do. If you're unsuccessful after five minutes, crate the dog again. Give her another chance to eliminate in fifteen or twenty minutes. Eventually, she will have to go.

Watch Your Pup

Be vigilant and don't let the pup make a mistake in the house. Each time you successfully anticipate elimination and take your pup to the potty spot, you'll move a step closer to your goal. Stay aware of your puppy's needs. If you ignore the pup, she will make mistakes and you'll be cleaning up more messes.

Keep a chart of your new dog's elimination behavior for the first three or four days. Jot down what times she eats, sleeps, and eliminates. After several days a pattern will emerge that can help you determine your pup's body rhythms. Most dogs tend to eliminate at fairly regular intervals. Once you know your new dog's natural rhythms, you'll be able to anticipate her needs and schedule appropriate potty outings.

Understanding the meanings of your dog's postures can also help you win the battle of the puddle. When your dog is getting ready to eliminate, she will display a specific set of postures. The sooner you can learn to read these signals, the cleaner your floor will stay.

A young puppy who feels the urge to eliminate may start to sniff the ground and walk in a circle. If the pup is very young, she may simply squat and go. All young puppies, male or female, squat to urinate. If you are housetraining a pup under 4 months of age, regardless of sex, watch for the beginnings of a squat as the signal to rush the pup to the potty area.

When a puppy is getting ready to defecate, she may run urgently back and forth or turn in a circle while sniffing or starting to squat. If defecation is imminent, the pup's anus may protrude or open slightly. When she starts to go, the pup will squat and hunch her back, her tail sticking straight out behind. There is no mistaking this posture; nothing else looks like this. If your pup takes this position, take her to her potty area. Hurry! You may have to carry her to get there in time.

There will come a time when your dog will be able to tell you when she needs to go out.

A young puppy won't have much time between feeling the urge and actually eliminating, so you'll have to be quick to note her postural clues and intercept your pup in time. Pups from 3 to 6 months have a few seconds more between the urge and the act than younger ones do. The older your pup, the more time you'll have to get her to the potty area after she begins the posture signals that alert you to her need.

Accidents Happen

If you see your pup about to eliminate somewhere other than the designated area, interrupt her immediately. Say "wait, wait, wait!" or clap your hands loudly to startle her into stopping. Carry the pup, if she's still small enough, or take her collar and lead her to the correct area. Once your dog is in the potty area, give her the command to eliminate. Use a friendly voice for the command, then wait patiently for her to produce. The pup may be tense because you've just startled her and may have to relax a bit before she's able to eliminate. When she does her job, include the command word in the praise you give ("good potty").

The old-fashioned way of housetraining involved punishing a dog's mistakes even before she knew what she was supposed to do. Puppies were punished for

It's not fair to expect a puppy to be able to control herself the way an adult dog can.

breaking rules they didn't understand about functions they couldn't control. This was not fair. While your dog is new to housetraining, there is no need or excuse for punishing her mistakes. Your job is to take the dog to the potty area just before she needs to go, especially with pups under 3 months old. If you aren't watching your pup closely enough and she has an accident, don't punish the puppy for your failure to anticipate her needs. It's not the pup's fault; it's yours.

In any case, punishment is not an effective tool for housetraining most dogs. Many will react to punishment by hiding puddles and feces where you won't find them right away (like behind the couch or under the desk). This eventually may lead to punishment after the fact, which leads to more hiding, and so on.

Instead of punishing for mistakes, stay a step ahead of potty accidents by learning to anticipate your pup's needs. Accompany your dog to the designated potty area when she needs to go. Tell her what you want her to do and praise her when she goes. This will work wonders. Punishment won't be necessary if you are a good teacher.

What happens if you come upon a mess after the fact? Some trainers say a dog can't remember having eliminated, even a few moments after she has done so. This is not true. The fact is that urine and feces carry a dog's unique scent, which she (and every other dog) can instantly recognize. So, if you happen upon a potty mistake after the fact you can still use it to teach your dog.

But remember, no punishment! Spanking, hitting, shaking, or scaring a puppy for having a housetraining accident is confusing and counterproductive. Spend your energy instead on positive forms of teaching.

Take your pup and a paper towel to the mess. Point to the urine or feces and calmly tell your puppy, "no potty here." Then scoop or sop up the accident with the paper towel. Take the evidence and the pup to the approved potty area. Drop the mess on the ground and tell the dog, "good potty here," as if she had done the deed in the right place. If your pup sniffs at the evidence, praise her calmly. If the accident happened very recently your dog may not have to go yet, but wait with her a few minutes anyway. If she eliminates, praise her. Afterwards, go finish cleaning up the mess.

Soon the puppy will understand that there is a place where you are pleased about elimination and other places where you are not. Praising for elimination in the approved place will help your pup remember the rules.

Scheduling Basics

With a new puppy in the home, don't be surprised if your rising time is suddenly a little earlier than you've been accustomed to. Puppies have earned a reputation as very early risers. When your pup wakes you at the crack of dawn, you will have to get up and take her to her elimination spot. Be patient. When your dog is an adult, she may enjoy sleeping in as much as you do.

At the end of the chapter, you'll find a typical housetraining schedule for puppies aged 10 weeks to 6 months. (To find schedules for younger and older pups, and for adult dogs, visit this book's companion web site.) It's fine to adjust the rising times when using this schedule, but you should not adjust the intervals between feedings and potty outings unless your pup's behavior justifies a change. Your puppy can only meet your expectations in housetraining if you help her learn the rules.

The schedule for puppies is devised with the assumption that someone will be home most of the time with the pup. That would be the best scenario, of course, but is not always possible. You may be able to ease the problems of a latchkey pup by having a neighbor or friend look in on the pup at noon and take her to eliminate. A better solution might be hiring a pet sitter to drop by midday. A professional pet sitter will be knowledgeable about companion animals and can give your pup high-quality care and socialization. Some can even help train your pup in both potty manners and basic obedience. Ask your veterinarian and your dog-owning friends to recommend a good pet sitter.

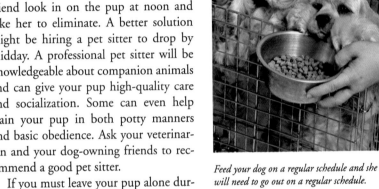

Feed your dog on a regular schedule and she will need to go out on a regular schedule.

If you must leave your pup alone during her early housetraining period, be sure to cover the entire floor of her corral with thick layers of overlapping newspaper. If you come home to messes in the puppy corral, just clean them up. Be patient—she's still a baby.

Use this schedule (and the ones on the companion web site) as a basic plan to help prevent housetraining accidents. Meanwhile, use your own powers of observation to discover how to best modify the basic schedule to fit your dog's unique needs. Each dog is an individual and will have her own rhythms, and each dog is reliable at a different age.

Schedule for Pups 10 Weeks to 6 Months

7:00 a.m.	Get up and take the puppy from her sleeping crate to her potty spot.
7:15	Clean up last night's messes, if any.
7:30	Food and fresh water.
7:45	Pick up the food bowl. Take the pup to her potty spot; wait and praise.
8:00	The pup plays around your feet while you have your breakfast.

continues

Schedule for Pups 10 Weeks to 6 Months (continued)

9:00	Potty break (younger pups may not be able to wait this long).
9:15	Play and obedience practice.
10:00	Potty break.
10:15	The puppy is in her corral with safe toys to chew and play with.
11:30	Potty break (younger pups may not be able to wait this long).
11:45	Food and fresh water.
12:00 p.m.	Pick up the food bowl and take the pup to her potty spot.
12:15	The puppy is in her corral with safe toys to chew and play with.
1:00	Potty break (younger pups may not be able to wait this long).
1:15	Put the pup on a leash and take her around the house with you.
3:30	Potty break (younger pups may not be able to wait this long).
3:45	Put the pup in her corral with safe toys and chews for solitary play and/or a nap.
4:45	Potty break.
5:00	Food and fresh water.
5:15	Potty break.
5:30	The pup may play nearby (either leashed or in her corral) while you prepare your evening meal.
7:00	Potty break.
7:15	Leashed or closely watched, the pup may play and socialize with family and visitors.
9:15	Potty break (younger pups may not be able to wait this long).
10:45	Last chance to potty.
11:00	Put the pup to bed in her crate for the night.

Appendix

Learning More About Your Cocker Spaniel

Some Good Books

About Cockers

Austin, Norman A., *The Complete American Cocker Spaniel,* Howell Book House, 1993.

Beauchamp, Richard, *American Cocker Spaniel,* Interpet Publishing, 2000.

Grossman, Alvin, *The American Cocker Spaniel,* 2nd ed., Doral Publishing, 2000.

About Health Care

Arden, Darlene, *The Angell Memorial Animal Hospital Book of Wellness and Preventive Care for Dogs,* Contemporary Books, 2003.

Eldredge, Debra M. DVM, Liisa D. Carlson, DVM, Delbert G. Carlson, DVM, James Giffin, MD, *Dog Owner's Home Veterinary Handbook,* 4th ed., Howell Book House, 2007.

Goldstein, Robert S., VMD, and Susan J. Goldstein, *The Goldsteins' Wellness and Longevity Program,* TFH Publications, 2005.

Messonnier, Shawn, DVM, *Eight Weeks to a Healthy Dog,* Rodale Books, 2003.

About Training

McCullough, Susan, *Housetraining for Dummies,* John Wiley and Sons, 2002.
Palika, Liz, *All Dogs Need Some Training,* Howell Book House, 1997.
Palika, Liz. *The KISS Guide to Raising a Puppy,* Dorling Kindersley, 2002.
Smith, Cheryl, *The Rosetta Bone,* Howell Book House, 2004.

Dog Sports and Activities

Davis, Kathy Diamond, *Therapy Dogs,* Howell Book House, 1992.
Deeley, Martin, *Working Gundogs: An Introduction to Training and Handling,* 2nd ed., Crowood Press, 1993.
Owens Wright, Sue, *150 Activities for Bored Dogs: Surefire Ways to Keep Your Dog Active and Happy,* Adams Media, 2007.
Palika, Liz, *The Complete Idiot's Guide to Dog Tricks,* Alpha Books, 2005.
Rawlings, Paul, *Gundog Training for the Home or Field,* Crowood Press, 2007.

Magazines

AKC Gazette
260 Madison Ave.
New York, NY 10016
www.akc.org/pubs/index.cfm

Bloodlines
100 East Kilgore Rd.
Kalamazoo, MI 49002
www.ukcdogs.com

Dog Fancy
P.O. Box 37185
Boone, IA 50037-0185
www.dogfancy.com

Dog World
P.O. Box 37185
Boone, IA 50037-0185
www.dogworldmag.com

Spaniels in the Field
P.O. Box 1737
New York, NY 10021
www.spanielsinthefield.com

Clubs and Registries

American Spaniel Club
Kathleen Patterson, ASC Secretary
PO Box 4194
Frankfort, KY 40604-4194
Asc.secretary@gmail.com
www.asc-cockerspaniel.org
This is the national club for the breed; its web site has a great deal of information, including upcoming shows and competitions. There are also many all-breed, individual breed, canine sport, and other special-interest dog clubs across the country. The registries listed below can help you find clubs in your area.

American Kennel Club
260 Madison Ave.
New York, NY 10016
(212) 696-8200
www.akc.org

Canadian Kennel Club
200 Ronson Dr.
Etobicoke, Ontario
Canada M9W 5Z9
(800) 250-8040 or (416) 675-5511
www.ckc.ca

United Kennel Club
100 East Kilgore Rd.
Kalamazoo, MI 49002
(616) 343-9020
www.ukcdogs.com

On the Internet

All About Cocker Spaniels

American Cocker Spaniel Rescue
www.americancockerspanielrescue.com
All about American Cocker Spaniel Rescue, including dogs who need homes and fund-raising efforts for the organization and the dogs in need.

American Cocker Spaniel Club Health News
www.asc-cockerspaniel.org/index.php/health/health-news.html
This site has information on Cocker health, from ongoing problems to new research being conducted in various fields.

American Cocker Spaniel Health Problems
www.mycockerspaniel.com/am_cocker_health.htm
Cocker Spaniel health information.

Cockers in the Field
www.fieldcockers.com
All about Cocker Spaniel field trials, including AKC trials, Spaniel Hunt Tests, and more.

Spaniel Field Trials
www.akc.org/events/field_trials/spaniels/history.cfm
An informative history of Cocker Spaniel field trials, including the breed's relationship with English Springer Spaniel field trials.

Versatile Cockers
www.versatilecockers.com
A showcase of talented Cocker Spaniels: conformation show dogs, agility dogs, obedience dogs, and more.

Canine Health

American Animal Hospital Association
www.healthypet.com
If you want to check out veterinary hospitals in your area, the American Animal Hospital Association web site provides a database of AAHA-accredited veterinary hospitals. The site also provides information about vaccinations, pain management, and parasite protection.

American College of Veterinary Internal Medicine
www.acvim.org
The American College of Veterinary Internal Medicine has a database of veterinary specialists, including cardiology, neurology, and oncology, searchable by area.

American Holistic Veterinary Medicine Association
www.ahvma.org
If you're looking for a holistic veterinarian, the American Holistic Veterinary Medical Association has a database of veterinarians in your area. The site also provides information on holistic modalities.

American Veterinary Medical Association
www.avma.org
The American Veterinary Medical Association web site with a wealth of information for dog owners, from disaster preparedness to both common and rare diseases affecting canines. There is also information on choosing the right dog and dog bite prevention.

Canine Health Information Center
www.caninehealthinfo.org
The Canine Health Information Center is a centralized canine health database jointly sponsored by the American Kennel Club Canine Health Foundation and the Orthopedic Foundation for Animals.

Dog Sports and Activities

Canine Freestyle Federation
www.canine-freestyle.org
This site is devoted to canine freestyle—dancing with your dog. There's information about freestyle events, tips, and even music!

Delta Society
www.deltasociety.org
The Delta Society promotes the human-animal bond through pet-assisted therapy and other programs.

Dog Patch
www.dogpatch.org
Information on many different dog sports and activities, including herding, agility, and Frisbee.

Dog Play
www.dog-play.com
More about dog sports and activities, including hiking, backpacking, therapy dog work, and much more.

Travel

Dog Friendly
www.dogfriendly.com
This web site publishes worldwide pet travel guides for dogs of all sizes and breeds. It includes information about dog-friendly events, attractions, resorts, vacation homes, and ski and beach locales throughout North America. Dog owners can benefit from the storm evacuation guide, tips on road trip preparation and travel etiquette, and even dog-friendly apartments.

Pets Welcome
www.petswelcome.com
Lists more than 25,000 hotels, B&Bs, ski resorts, campgrounds, and beaches that are pet-friendly. It even has listings you can download onto your GPS (global pooch system). The site supplies travel tips and blogs on travel recommendations for dog owners.

Photo Credits:
Isabelle Francais: 1, 4–5, 8–9, 11, 12, 14, 15, 18, 19, 20, 22, 23, 25, 26, 27, 30, 32, 33, 34, 37, 38, 44, 48, 50 (*top*), 52, 53, 55, 57, 58, 60, 63, 64, 65, 68, 69, 70, 71, 76, 79, 84, 85, 90, 91, 93, 95, 100–101, 124, 125, 127, 131, 133
Bonnie Nance: 16
Tammy Raabe Rao/rubicat.com: 24, 28, 35, 41, 42–43, 45, 50 (*bottom*), 54, 62, 75, 78, 82, 97, 99, 102, 122, 128, 130
Howell Book House: 10, 110, 111, 113, 114, 115, 117, 118, 119, 120

Index

adult dog, choosing, 34, 41
allergies, 75
American Kennel Club (AKC), 12, 13, 21–23
American Spaniel Club, 23
anal sac problems, 76
antifreeze poisoning, 92
appearance, breed standard for, 12–15
ascarids, 89
ASPCA Animal Poison Control Center, 96
attention, training, 118–120
autoimmune diseases, 76

baby gates, 123
back, breed standard for, 13
barking, 48
bathing, 66
bee stings, 92
behavior problems, 26, 31, 44–45, 54
bites, treating, 93
biting by dog, 23, 27, 30, 31, 49
bleeding, controlling, 93
body, breed standard for, 12–13
body language, 111
bonding, 52
breeder
    backyard, 33–34
    housetraining by, 122
    questions from, 36–37
    reputable, 33
breeding, 88
breed standard, 12–15
bringing your dog home, 52
brushing, 63–64
burns, 93

calculus, 85–86
character, of breed, 15–17
cherry eye, 77–78
chest, breed standard for, 13
chewing, 45, 54
chew toys, 51
children, 16–17, 26–27
chocolate toxicosis, 93
choke chain, 109
choking, 94
choosing your Cocker Spaniel
    adult dog, 34, 41
    finding the right dog for you, 36–37
    puppies, 37–40
    where to get your Cocker, 32–36
cleanup supplies, 123, 124
clicker, training use of, 111
clippers, 68–71
coat
    breed standard, 14–15
    colors, 14–15
    examination, 86–87
    grooming, 63–71
colitis, 76
collar, 50, 51, 109
colors, 14–15
combing, 63–66
come command, 115–116
commands
    come, 115–116
    down, 113–114
    for elimination, 124, 126, 131
    let's go, 117–118
    OK, 113
    sit, 112–113
    stay, 114–115

companions, Cockers as, 16–17
conjunctivitis, 78
cooperation, teaching, 121
corral, puppy, 126–127
crate
    housetraining use, 53, 125–126
    overuse of, 125
    selecting, 51, 53
    types, 53, 123

dewclaws, 13
digging, 48, 49
dishes, food and water, 51
down command, 113–114
drowning, 95
dry eye, 78–79

ears
    breed standard, 14
    cleaning, 66
    examination, 85
    health problems, 76–77
electrocution, 95
emergency care, 92–97
English Cocker Spaniel, 11, 19–23
English Springer Spaniel, 11, 19–20
enzymatic cleaner, 124
epilepsy, 82
exercise, need for, 28
exercise pen, 124
expression, breed standard for, 14
eye contact, 119
eye examination, 84–85
eye problems
    blocked tear ducts, 77
    cherry eye, 77–78
    conjunctivitis, 78
    dry eye, 78–79

feathering, 14, 28
fence, 48–49
flea allergy dermatitis, 72, 79
fleas
    checking for, 71–72
    controlling in environment, 72–73
    preventives, 67

food
    amount to feed, 60
    commercial, 57–58
    free feeding, 59–60
    homemade, 58
    ingredients, 58, 59
    labels, 59
    mealtimes, 61–62
    people, 61–62
    recall, 57–58
    treats, 62

gait, 15
geriatric care, 98–99
giardia, 90
groomer, 56
grooming
    bathing, 66
    brushing, 63–64
    clipping/trimming, 68–71
    ear cleaning, 66
    mat removal, 65–66
    nail care, 67–68
    professional, 56
    requirements, 27–28
    tools, 51, 65, 68
gum color, checking, 84

head, breed standard for, 14, 22
health issues. See also specific disorders
    emergency care, 92–97
    geriatric care, 98–99
    recognizing normal health, 83–89
    when to call the veterinarian, 86–87
hearing, 27, 98
heart rate, 84
heartworms, 90
heatstroke, 95
height, 12
hip dysplasia, 79
history, of breed, 18–23
home
    flea control, 72
    puppy-proofing, 44–47
hookworm, 90–91

housetraining
  accidents, 130–132
  anticipating need to eliminate, 129–130
  by breeder, 122
  charting elimination behavior, 129
  cleanup, 123, 124, 128, 132
  crate use, 53, 125–126
  elimination area, 124–130
  first day, 124–126
  indoor to outdoor switching techniques, 127–129
  by mother dog, 122
  newspaper use, 123, 127–128
  pet sitter, 133
  punishment, 131–132
  puppy corral use, 126–127
  scent marker, 127
  schedule, 132–134
  shopping list, 122–124
  water access, 126
hunting, 12, 16, 18–19
hypothyroidism, 82–83

identification, 50
insect growth regulators (IGRs), 67
interdigital cysts, 80

leadership, 104
leash
  introduction to, 110
  selecting, 51
  for training, 109
legs, breed standard for, 13
let's go command, 117–118
life span, 32
lip fold pyoderma, 81
luxating patella, 82

marker, positive, 111–112
mats, 27, 56, 65–66
mouth examination, 85–86

nail care, 67–68
nail cutters, 51
name, choosing, 50, 52
neck, breed standard for, 13

neutering, 88
newspaper, housetraining use, 123, 127–128
nose
  color, 14
  examination, 87

obesity, 28, 62
OK command, 113
origin, of breed, 19–20
ownership
  evaluating readiness for, 24–25
  requirements, 31

parasites
  external, 71–74
  internal, 89–92
patella, luxating, 82
pet sitter, 133
plastic bags, for poop removal, 123
play, training during, 104–105
poisoning, 96
poop removal tools, 123
popularity, of breed, 23
positive reinforcement, 104, 105, 106
puddle pads, housetraining use, 123
pulse, 84
punishment, 104, 105–107, 108, 131–132
puppy
  choosing, 37–40
  evaluating litter, 38–39
  housetraining, 122–134
  socialization, 30
  supplies, 51
  temperament test, 40
  training, 17
  vaccines, 80–81
puppy-proofing your home, 44–47

recall, training techniques, 116
release word/prompt, 104, 112, 113, 114–115, 119
remote consequences, 107–109
reproductive system health, 89
rescue groups, 34, 36
reward, training, 104, 105, 106

roundworms, 89
routine, desire for, 27

scent marker, 127
schedule, housetraining, 132–134
seborrhea, ear margin, 77
seizures, 82, 96–97
senses, 27
separation anxiety, 48
shampoo, 66
shelters, obtaining dog from, 34–35
shock, 97
sit command, 112–113
skin, examination of, 86
skunk spray, 97
sleeping habits, 27
smell, sense of, 27, 45
socialization, 30
social rank, 103–104
spaniels, 11, 18–20
spaying, 88
stay command, 114–115
stress, chronic, 16
supervision of dog, 54
supplies
    basic, 49, 51
    cleanup, 123, 124
    grooming tools, 51, 65, 68

tag, ID, 50
tail, breed standard for, 13
tapeworms, 91
taste, sense of, 27
tear ducts, blocked, 77
temperament, 23, 35, 40
temperature, taking, 83–84
tethering, training technique, 110–111
thyroid disease, 82–83
ticks, 73, 74
time commitment, 54–55
touch, sense of, 27
toys, 51, 104, 109
trainability, 17
trainer, 56
training
    attention, 118–120
    benefits of, 102

canine nature, 103
come command, 115–116
cooperation, 121
crate use, 53
down command, 113–114
equipment, 109
how dogs learn, 105
leadership, 104
leash introduction, 110
let's go command, 117–118
life's rewards, 105
OK command, 113
during play, 105
positive marker, 111–112
positive reinforcement, 104, 105, 106
punishment, 104, 105–107, 108
recall command, 116
remote consequences, 107–109
sit command, 112–113
stay command, 114–115
tethering, 110–111
versatility of Cockers, 30
treasure hunt, training game, 119–120
treats, 62
tug of war, aggressiveness from, 104

urinary system health, 89

vaccine reactions, 83
vaccines, 80–81
veterinarian
    selecting, 55–56
    when to call, 86–87
vision, 27, 98
von Willebrand's disease, 83

water, 49, 126
weight, 12
whipworms, 91–92
worms, 89–92

yard
    flea control, 73
    puppy-proofing, 47
    safety, 48–49